Second Act

Living Boldly and Abundantly at Every Age

CHERI SYPHAX

This work reflects actual events in the life of the author as truthfully as recollection permits. Some events have been compressed, and some dialogue has been recreated. While all persons within are actual individuals, names and identifying characteristics have been changed to protect their privacy.

Copyright 2022 by Cheri Syphax

All rights reserved. No part of this book may be reproduced or used in any manner without written permission of the copyright owner except for the use of quotations in a book review.

For more information, address:
cheri@phaxmarketingsolutions.com

Paperback ISBN: 979-8-9871356-0-0
Ebook ISBN: 979-8-9871356-1-7
Hardcover ISBN: 979-8-9871356-2-4
www.phaxmarketingsolutions.com

Dedication:

To all of the women who are in transition, who are unsure, have had hurdles, or challenges, have felt awkward, invisible, or lack confidence, been abused, misused, or are menopausal, whatever it is, know that a whole other life is on the other side of doubt or fear. Trust yourself, trust the process, be open to doing the work, and realize an amazing Second Act can be waiting for you.

Contents

Dedication: iii

Introduction: To Have and To Hold.................................... 1

Chapter 1: A Breath of Knowledge...................................... 7

Chapter 2: Non-Conformist.. 21

Chapter 3: Grown Woman.. 40

Chapter 4: Through the Storm.. 54

Chapter 5: Rebirth 67

Chapter 6: To Those I've Tried to Please... 81

Chapter 7: Divine Timing... 99

Chapter 8: Higher Ground.. 112

Chapter 9: Liberation is Liberating 126

Chapter 10: Believers Keep On Believin' 143

Chapter 11: The Golden Year 164

Chapter 12: It's Our Turn... 184

Acknowledgements:.. 197

INTRODUCTION

To Have and To Hold

As soon as Jamie Foxx's sultry voice crooned the lyrics to "When I First Saw You," I knew that was my cue. Some 80 pairs of eyes focused on me as I emerged into view. I paused at the top of the staircase. Standing on the balcony, I caught a glimpse of familiar faces organized neatly into a circular formation, their joy radiating towards me. Despite having all the attention of everyone in the room, I tune out most of it. But I can't help but notice the two empty chairs among the faction.

Holding a small bouquet of white roses in my left hand, I extended my right and wrapped my palm around the top of the railing. I took a breath and began my stride down the stairs.

Cheri, don't fall!

I extended one foot forward. And then the other.

Take one step down. Repeat. Step down. Do it again.

My hand is still positioned on the cool, steel railing. It is my support mechanism to balance myself as I continued my descent down nearly four dozen stairs. I kept my head lifted high, alternating between smiling at the photographers in my path and bracing myself not to break down in tears.

If I look at Tracey, I can get through this.

Jamie continues to croon in the background about when he first sets eyes on the woman of his dreams.

Never have I felt so regal. My makeup? Flawless. Hair, meticulously slicked into a high bun with a jeweled headband. And my dress, white and stunning, with intricate craftsmanship of lace and beading, handmade by women from Uganda with a low plunging neckline and a sheer nude mesh covering my chest, a physical armor proudly displaying hints of survival and renewal. In the back, a modest open circle, exposing a section of my honey brown skin between my shoulder blades.

I turned my head to look in the direction of my soon-to-be husband, standing next to the minister. Our eyes connected, and our smiles met. I winked.

Back to these stairs. One step and then another.

What felt like a walk for eternity lasted for two and a half minutes. I was at the bottom of the stairway by the time Jamie finished the song, belting out a final *dreeeeaaaammm*. Giving my hand to my brother, he guided me through the final leg of my trek. My sight stayed concentrated on the man at the end of my path as I passed through a sea of eyes and phones snapping pictures. Then at last, the distance between us shrunk, and finally, I was standing across from him at the altar. His chestnut eyes sparkled through his glasses as he flashed his charming smile, the one that makes my heart jump every time.

I took a second to compose myself. Inhale. His energy, a sense of peace and serenity, overrides my jitters and anxiousness. In the days and hours leading up to that moment, everything was a blur. I had to move from one thing to the next. Another task to check off the list. A different inquiry to solve. More people to greet.

None of that matters now.

My eyes go up and meet his. I smile back.

This is finally happening.

Tracey is probably the closest thing to perfection that I've ever experienced in my life. He walked into it a little over one year ago from this day. Or more like slid into it. Unbeknownst to me, 2020 had other plans. Being 50 and single, the last thing I wanted was to be held hostage inside with little to no male interaction. Not appealing. So, for the first time, I turned to Match.com. Before then, I didn't feel the need to date online. Heck, I thought people were crazy, and I heard plenty of horror stories of dick pics and ghosting. My plan was to sign up, meet men, chat while we were inside, and move on. I was going in with zero expectations.

About a week or two in, my DM lit up with a notification. Clicking on the unread message, I noticed the profile picture of this handsome man, who wrote three simple words: "Welcome to Philadelphia!" (Come to find out, he didn't even live in Philly!)

Zoom and FaceTime calls. Zoom candlelit dinners. Zoom coffees. Zoom breakfasts. Endless nights of talking until 10 or 11 p.m. like high school teenagers who couldn't get enough of each other. We didn't want to leave the world we created for ourselves. Tracey and I exposed every ounce to each other. There were no pretenses, no faking. All of that goes out the window when you're dating in the middle of a global pandemic. He saw me in my bonnet, and I saw him after he cut himself shaving. He and I got to know each other straight up.

I guess it's true what they say – you can find love in unexpected places and when you least expect it.

How can this man be this perfect? I kept asking myself.

Standing in front of him – deliciously dressed in a sleek, black tux, black buttoned-up dress shirt and black tie – in this stunning museum, it was as if no one else was in the room. I could faintly hear the minister's voice, but my attention was on Tracey. It's just him and me, as it had been for the entire pandemic. Staring into each other's eyes. Smiles never leave our faces as we mouth *I love you* to one another. As much of a believer in romance as I am, I couldn't have imagined a feeling like this. We lock our right hands at the minister's behest, Tracey's thumb caressing the top of my palm and mine over his.

In finding the words for my vows to Tracey, I had to let him know, contrary to the things that I first told him I would never do for someone, that all changed with him. That's how I knew he was the one for me. The right person turns all of those "I won't dos" on its head.

... [to] the man I told I don't cook but inspires me to cook lunch and dinner regularly. The man I told that I love Philly and would never leave, but has moved me to Trenton. The man who has me looking forward to working out when working out is not my thing...

I didn't realize it, but for every failed relationship and test that life has thrown at me was all to prepare me for him.

...[to] the man who calms my soul, and the man who prays with me. The man who meditates with me, and works deliberately at communicating effectively with me. The man who knows my love language and speaks it daily. The man who gently whispers in my ear how much he loves me. The man who is silly and keeps me laughing. The man who lets me be me and loves all of my uniqueness...

As each word flowed from my lips, I looked at Tracey, his head focused, listening intently. Then finishing my love letter to him, with thunderous applause in the background, he lifted his head and said three simple words: "All of that."

When he started his pledge to me with, "As you know, I love you, right?" a giggle escaped my body. Caught up in his velvety tone as he continued to recite his vows, I knew every word that left his mouth came deep down from his soul.

He loves me.

He adores me.

As our lips touched, so soft and warm, I felt my desire for him in every cell of my being. Every obstacle, every triumph — they all brought me to this moment. Finally, I am Mrs. Cheri Syphax.

At that moment, Tracey and I became one. But to come together, I had to release the weight of that which no longer served me, even before I filled out my dating profile. In life, everything we endure prepares us for our subsequent chapter—the next act. For so long, I carried the heaviness of my past and fears, subscribing to living within the confines I set for myself. Until I chose to reevaluate my life and ask myself, *what's prevented me from reaching that next level?* The answer was me.

Now that I'm in my golden decade, I can tell you that I don't have all the answers. But what I do have, and want to share with you, is that every challenge or down moment does not have to define you. In contrast, they're opportunities for growth and transformation. Or a chance to rewrite your story. There are truths I've had to face and reconcile with to confidently design my life on my terms and authentically live in my truth. And that required taking risks like beginning a new career at 45, moving across the country, and opening my heart to the possibility of a second chance at love.

This is my wish for you. To get out of your own way so that you, too, can have the love and the life you deserve.

CHAPTER 1

A Breath of Knowledge

For some people, their most treasured childhood memories are anchored by one or two places. Like the home they spent their formative years, where summers meant extended hours playing outside until dusk, catching the tantalizing aroma of grilled foods, or splashing around in a pool or lake.

That wasn't always the case for me.

My early years are defined by a juxtaposition of cultures, social movements, locations, and individuals. To this day, I'm not entirely sure what home feels like, as I bounced from one set of people to another. I wasn't a military brat, yet I was brought up to be a global citizen and a daughter of the land. Growing up, what I knew for certain was I was wrapped up in so much love.

I was born in California on January 26, 1970, as the only child of two high school seniors, Sonja Spigner and Quincey Newsome. I don't know much about my mother's pregnancy or the conditions of my arrival. But knowing how my maternal grandparents were Southern Baptists, I doubt they were happy to find out their teenage child was pregnant. You may think having a kid would've slowed my mother down - quite the opposite. If there's anything I know about Sonja, she was a bit of a rebel back then. And that extended to her pregnancy. I have a cousin on my mother's side who is one month older than me. My aunt hid her pregnancy until the very end. Sonja, on the other hand, shrugged it off. "They gon' know anyway," I can imagine her saying. Even now, I still don't know how she told my grandparents. But that was Sonja. Walking to the beat of her own drum.

At birth, my mother gave me four names, each chosen deliberately to represent a link to culture and ancestry. The first is Yolaroza, which is either Yoruba or Swahili for rainbow. It's fitting since my personality is very colorful, and I am known to bring a lot of sunshine into people's lives! The second, Cheri, stands for my dear in French (mom believed we had some of that nationality in our family). Next is DeVaugh, and last, Spigner, for my mother's maiden name. I wasn't given my father's last name because his mother lived by the Holiness faith. She couldn't fathom the idea of her son having sex. This may seem like my pending arrival would make for a tension-filled beginning, especially since two teenagers had a child out of wedlock. But by the time I came along, it was all love between everyone.

Although my mother was in high school when she gave birth to me, it didn't stop her from going directly to Arizona State University (ASU). In my family, education was a fact of life. It wasn't something that she or my grandparents sat me down to discuss why I should take it seriously and pursue it. I think we often pick up things through osmosis. There was always an emphasis on being able to read and ask questions. Simply put,

SECOND ACT

I was surrounded by people who made learning as important as breathing.

My maternal great-grandparents are said to have been sharecroppers, if not enslaved people, and grew up at a time when they couldn't learn how to read. As for my maternal and paternal grandparents, reading was a thing that wasn't as accessible in their earlier years. For my folks, getting an education was the crème de la crème. The value I was brought up on was that no matter what, no one could take your education away from you. Nowadays, it sometimes feels like we, as Black people, don't have the same desire for education, especially considering how it was once denied to us. Because it was elusive at one point, education was a non-negotiable in my family. My grandparents were teachers on a Navajo reservation in Chinle, Arizona, for some 20 or 30 years. They'd often get a lot of recognition from the community, especially from former students who returned to Chinle after finishing college to thank my grandparents for the role they played as educators. Between them and spending time with my mom on campus, the value of knowledge was deeply rooted in me. Growing up, I was super curious and could read by age three. So, it wasn't unusual for me to ask questions a lot, particularly, *why?*

While mom was away at Arizona State University (ASU), I lived with my grandparents about five hours away on the reservation. Located on the northern side of the state in Apache County, the Chinle region is inhabited by nearly 5,000 residents, according to 2019 census data. Today, it's known for being one of the main trading centers. Visitors from all over the world come to enjoy the nearby Canyon de Chelly National Monument, an 84,000-acre site that's preserved a rich collection of archaeological ruins from three Indigenous tribes – Pueblo, Hopi, and Navajo. However, once summer came, mom would pick me up, and we'd drive back to Tempe. Taking me with her to campus, I'd slip my pint-sized hand into hers and prance along at her side as we passed a formation of palm trees and students whisking past us on their bikes and skateboards.

I was immersed in Indigenous culture from the ages of three and five. I loved my time with my mom, but I always enjoyed being on the reservation. There was a simplicity to it. And honesty, nobody was trying to be anything but who and what they were. I think that's what I try to build in my life today. My days were filled with pristine skies and picturesque views of open lands extending as far as my eye could see. In the distance, my sightlines caught salmon-colored rock arches, mountains, and sandstone formations. It was routine to hear someone chanting along with the beating of a drum nearby. Outside with my grandparents, I'd pass by sweat houses, teepees, and artisan vendors making sand paintings and jewelry with turquoise. I can still imagine the scent of fry bread cooking, that tempting smell of oil mixing with flour. Celebrations were my favorite, especially sunrise services with cultural singing, dancing, and chanting, which took place during what many call Thanksgiving.

Yet no matter how humble life in Chinle was for me, the Indigenous community was not immune to fighting their own social justice battles at that time. The government had built bungalows to house people initially pushed off of their native land. I remember being in my grandparents' backyard, looking at the family that lived next to us and seeing the elders in thatched huts. In 1970, most families on the Navajo reservation lived in severe poverty. The typical house had just one or two rooms. It was reported that 60 percent of the reservation's dwellings had no electricity, and 80 percent had no running water or sewers. The education levels were also low, hence my grandparents' dedication. Looking back on the treatment and living conditions of the Indigenous people, this was my first introduction to the injustices of this country. Unknowingly, it set the foundation for my passion for equity.

Though my grandparents referred to each other as Matthew and Opal, they were Mama Opal and Daddy Matthew to me. In my mind, they were the best two people ever to walk this planet. Mama Opal was a strong and wise woman, considered tall at just over 5' 7", with small shoulders and a larger bottom. Her skin was yellow and her nose was sharp, she had a heart-shaped face and somewhat deep-set eyes. It almost looked like she was squinting when she got tired. Her hair was thick and jet black and would be pressed with Ultra Sheen hair grease. I'd often watch her sit at the vanity and roll up strands of her hair with pink sponge rollers and pieces of toilet paper or a brown paper bag.

When the three of us were together, Mama Opal had plenty to say; but outside of the house, she was quiet and kept to herself. She wasn't trusting of everyone, and I think a lot of that had to do with how she was raised. Her father was Black and white with a lighter complexion, while her mother was Indian and Black with a darker hue. Since the older generations are so against discussing any past traumas or emotional scars, I can only guess that not fitting in with anyone except her immediate family affected her ability to connect with people.

Daddy Matthew was a meek and humble soul. He wasn't big in stature; I would guess he was around 5'9" or 5'10". Carrying dominant negroid features, Daddy Matthew had a broad nose, very full lips, high-standing cheekbones and blue eyes. He was affectionately known as "head" because he had a big one - it's synonymous with the Spigner family because I have it too. He would attribute his head size to having a big brain. I've seen pictures of him when he had more weight on him, but most of my life, I remember him with a slight build and a contagious smile. While serving in the military, a bomb exploded on his face, giving him some skin discoloration near his eye.

Everyone loved Mr. Spigner. He was a deacon at the local church and coached baseball for the kids in the community. He was a striking, yet soft-spoken man. I never heard him raise his voice until he got Alzheimer's. He was the kind that would say something funny and have a good cackle at his own jokes. With him, neither myself, Mama Opal, nor my mother wanted for nothing, because he gave us everything. He displayed only the utmost respect for women. He'd clean around the house, wash clothes, and cook meals. He was the type to defer to his wife, even as the breadwinner of the house. Whenever I'd ask him for something, he'd always reply, "Go ask your mother."

While staying with them, my days usually started when Mama Opal awakened me by 7 a.m. to get ready for daycare. She'd help me get dressed, put on my favorite T-shirt and shorts, and then sit me down to do my hair. Her go-to style was separating my hair on each side, turning each into a single ponytail, complete with matching barrettes at the end of the braid. After eating a breakfast of fry bread and eggs, I'd leave the dining table and pick up my bookbag from my room. Then with Mama Opal guiding me out the front door, I'd walk over to the car in the driveway, waiting for her to meet me at the rear door so she could help buckle me in. Then it was off to daycare. When it was time to leave, my grandparents would alternate between picking me up. Once home, as one cooked dinner, I'd sit at the dining room table with the other, talking about my day as if I were grown. I'm not what some would call an old soul, but Mama Opal and Daddy Matthew certainly interacted with me like I was a young adult, for sure. Being raised in an older environment, I was exposed to whatever my grandparents talked about, watched, or listened to on the news. Since Mama Opal retired from teaching earlier than my grandfather, when I wasn't at daycare, we'd sit back and watch her favorite stories, *Days of Our Lives* and *The Young and The Restless*. (As a little girl, I knew far too much about Victor Newman!)

My grandparents had simplicity in the way they lived. It was a good life. They didn't try to impress anyone. They didn't try to live outside their means. It was all about what was happening inside our home. Such a contrast from being in California, where, for a while, I would get caught up in who's who and what things looked like. But as I continue to mature, I always return to the center of what's peace for me. And my grandparents had it. They had the perfect routine. In the mornings, Daddy Matthew would make coffee for the household while my grandmother was outside, hanging washed, damp clothes on the line. They would be done with honey do's and breakfast, just in time to catch the *Price is Right*. Their favorite game was Scrabble, and they had notebooks with words and definitions. Such brilliant people. If there were any question of where I got my enthusiasm for education and knowledge of random trivial facts, it'd be from them.

I don't remember my grandparents ever having any problems. They may have, but I wasn't privy to it. What's stayed with me about them is how they were a great team when it came to raising their children and also just super supportive. Above all, they taught me how to be a good person and treat people well. Although Mama Opal was judgmental, both of them just kind of let people do their thing. They brought me up to live with a lot of grace, respect, and dignity, and to give others kindness, too.

I didn't spend those earlier days with just my maternal grandparents. My time was also split with my paternal grandmother. After mom graduated from ASU, I was put on a plane headed back to the Bay, where I'd stay with my Grandma Lillie. (Mom stayed behind in Arizona to pick up the car Daddy Matthew gave her and start the 14-hour journey back to California.) Flying on my own was like going on an adventure, a young Cheri carrying an orange backpack full of belongings, with my name written on everything I owned. I remember the airline stewardess spoiling me with snacks and apple juice. This was back in the days before 9/11, when airlines gave out those miniature wings to pin on your shirt, and people could walk you to the gate or meet you when you got off the plane. When the flight landed, and the stewardess escorted me off, there was Grandma Lillie standing in the waiting area outside of the skybridge to pick me up.

A proud woman who walked with a slight bend at her waist, Grandma Lillie had striking features: strong cheekbones, beautiful brown skin, and salt and pepper hair. I've been told that she and her sisters migrated to California from Norfolk, Va, for work. I believe she fled to safety from my grandfather, whom I had never met. I don't know for a fact, but I strongly sense that she couldn't read. She'd often have me read to her – her mail, passages from the Bible, pretty much everything. An amazing Southern cook, my mouth still waters whenever I think about her standing over the stove, that sweet scent of apple and cinnamon filling the house. I don't know of anyone, except her sister, who could make homemade applesauce the way she did. In later years, spending time at Grandma Lillie's house also meant time with my two younger brothers – brothers from my father's new marriage.

My father was Grandma Lillie's only child, and she raised him as a single mother. Growing up, he was the little man of the house. Doted on by his mother and aunts, he had no accountability, and when I tell you, he was spoiled rotten! There was some contention initially between Grandma Lillie and my mother since mom proved that her cherished son was sexually active. But both women loved me so much, so it didn't matter. They just kind of dealt with each other.

***

The difference in personality and parenting styles between Mamma Opal and my mother indicated two generations coming to a head. It was all at a time when marginalized people – Black people, women, Native Americans, gays and lesbians, and folks with disabilities – were fighting for equality. Also, when the energy crisis, Vietnam War, and Watergate scandal competed for the world's attention. Momma Opal was submissive, but not in a weak way. She knew her place as a woman at home and within society. On the other hand, my mother was the epitome of "I'm Black, and I'm proud!" She stood around 5'8" and was somewhat pear-shaped like her mother. She had light brown sugar skin with orange undertones. Also, like her mother, her nose was somewhat sharp - but her lips were full, which she took after her father, and they matched the roundness of her face. She wore her hair in a short, but well-manicured afro when I was young but as she got older, she wore her hair short and relaxed (and later, blonde) - the perfect hairstyle to showcase her flawless skin. She was never one to back down from a debate or an argument. Sonja had to prove her point. In the 70s, with the culmination of various movements happening, my mother was front and center, especially when she became a member of the Black Panther Party for Self-Defense.

Looking back, I used to take after my mother. But later, I had to do some inventory on myself. One glaring distinction between the two women – mom, was single and never married. From what I observed when I was younger, some ways about my mother probably kept her from or uninterested in marriage. Momma Opal, alternatively, knew how to be married. My grandparents were together forever, practically, from the age of 14 until they passed in their 80s. What stands out most to me about their union is how there was a vulnerability to their relationship. It was a dance of giving and receiving, compromising with one another. When women ask me how to find love, I tell them there's nothing wrong with softening ourselves because I certainly have. But it doesn't mean it takes away from who you are. My mom was a single parent who worked hard every day. Though Momma Opal worked as a teacher, her lifestyle was unlike that of her daughter. She wasn't raising children alone; she had a partner to do it with, and so her stress level was low.

Still, there wasn't anything my mom wouldn't do for me, including feeding my wanderlust. My fascination for travel developed early, from living on the reservation and going on road trips with my grandparents between California and Tyler, Texas, where they also had a home. One of my favorite trips with my mom was to Honolulu and Waikiki Beach. While there, we went to a luau and did a cruise. I got so sick that I thought I would be seasick forever. We also went to a zoo, where I remember standing next to a parakeet and wondering if it was going to attack me with its beak. On that trip, I was the only child amongst a group of adults. So mom was already grooming me for future adventures.

Like her parents, Mom was also a teacher. She had a master's in special education but never worked in the classroom. Instead, she was a curriculum specialist for a community organization. That meant she was super involved with my schooling. Of course, like any child, I'd test boundaries with my teachers, and my mom would defend me until the cows came home. I remember in high school when I used to cut my typing class. No reason. I just did, probably because I felt great about my ability. I knew how to type well, but the class was a requirement. If you had an unexcused absence, your grade would be knocked down. I had a few absences for cutting class, so instead of having an 'A,' I was getting an 'F.' On a Wednesday afternoon, my mother marched into my school to the principal's office to see about the situation.

"I don't care if she hasn't been in class," she said, a matter of factly. "Can she type?"

"Yes."

That's all she needed to hear. "Then she better get an 'A!'"

That was my mother – super intelligent and no-nonsense. She played no games! With her, there was closeness and security. I felt empowered and supported by her.

Even though we didn't have much when it came to money, she made sure that I had the best. That meant sending me to Kensington, an all-white school in an affluent enclave in Berkeley Hills overlooking the San Francisco Bay. In 1968, Berkeley kicked off what was considered a "pioneering" busing plan to integrate the city's public schools fully. Though other school districts across the country had previously instituted varying integration efforts before 1968, Berkeley was recognized as the first city to take up its busing program voluntarily. The arrangement was organized as two-way busing. Black kids got transported to predominantly white schools, and white children were bussed to primarily Black schools, all in the name of educational equality. My mother's decision to send me to a white school was based on education. Period.

I started attending at six years old when I was in the first grade. Every weekday, I'd wake at 6 a.m. to get ready and head out in time to catch the yellow school bus for the 20-minute journey away from home. To me, that time was nothing but fun. For us kids, it was as if we had our own little tribe embarking on this trek together to what was like another world. A few months later, funding was cut by the school district, so my mother switched to public transport for my daily commute. I traded in my yellow bus adventure for a crowded, one-hour journey on the AC Transit bus to get to school. It still didn't matter to me. Being on my own, using public transportation – you couldn't tell me nothing. I was grown!

Every day, it was as if I stepped in and out of two different realms. By day, I went what felt pretty far away to the Hills. At night, I ventured home to Crescent Park, also known as the flatlands, or flats for short, on the Bay's east side. A mostly Black area, but there was also a bit of Hispanic and Filipino mixed in. Though it's designated public housing by West Coast standards, Crescent Park is not what people typically think of when they hear "the projects." Unlike East Coast housing, which to me resembles prisons with towering brick buildings, Crescent Park had garden apartments within cul de sacs. Its square buildings had a maximum of two stories, contrasting the multi-floor structures in Chicago or the boroughs of New York City. Still, this was in the late 70s and 80s, and what was identical between East and West Coast public housing were the conditions surrounding them. There were drugs, prostitution, and drive-by shootings outside our front door. Of course, being my inquisitive self, curiosity peaked about what was happening out there. But mom insisted on keeping me away from the temptations lurking beyond our door and did not allow me to go outside to play with the other kids. When I came home from school, my chores were homework and cooking dinner so that it would be ready by the time she walked through the door.

As one of the few Black kids at school, I was regularly invited to my classmates' houses. And I enjoyed it. Looking back on that time, I think it showed how innocent children are. As adults, we assign more to things than necessary. For me, visiting their homes was like being transported to another world. Those residences in the Hills were mixed - some large, others smaller, but they all had spacious front and back yards. It starkly contrasted my reality of living in a cramped, two-bedroom apartment with no backyard. It wasn't as if I'd never experienced those spaces before. After they retired, Mama Opal and Daddy Matthew had a nice-sized rancher, which they had built in Tyler, Texas. And my other relatives, who were considered middle class, had homes designed for the typical nuclear family. To be transparent, I can't say that I always felt comfortable going to my white friends' house because no one came to mine. But even so, I never felt ashamed of where mom raised me.

For as far back as I can remember, I was groomed to navigate different spaces. The Navajo reservation. A college campus. Public housing. A predominantly white school. Summers in the south. I don't mark these places as home. It's the people and the relationships I developed that left an impression on me. This was my foundation. It was the beginning of my journey of learning how to assert my place in the world and uncover who exactly Cheri was.

CHAPTER 2

Non-Conformist

Sonja Spigner was as sophisticated as she was audacious. What's more, she emitted a certain gravitas that let people know she was a poised and intelligent woman who wasn't afraid to speak her mind. Transitioning into adulthood during the rise of social progressivism – a time when feminism challenged the role of women in society – my mother had a strong sense of self. She was remarkably steadfast about whatever it was she believed in. But the qualities I admired most about her would later become the same ones that led to my resenting her.

With my mother's formative years occurring during the 1960s, it's not hard to connect the dots about how she became the person she was. The '60s laid the groundwork for the radical and militant atmosphere of the '70s. It saw the expansion of the middle class, and the decade began with lofty claims of initiatives, legislation, and programs to combat poverty and racial injustice. Yet what really came to define that era was the emergence of the counterculture. Or the anti-establishment phenomenon that saw the growth of various lifestyles and ideologies like the rise of the hippie, second-wave feminism, and the sexual revolution. It was also about dozens of social and political movements, including anti-war, gay rights, Asian American, Chicano, and Black Civil Rights.

By 1970, there was a restlessness in the air over failed promises of reform and equality that spilled over from the previous decade. For Black people, the anger and frustration that true equality had not come to pass sparked the Black Power revolutionary movement. It emphasized pride in ourselves, economic empowerment, and the creation of political and cultural institutions. At the same time, we leaned all the way into celebrating the essence of who we were as Black Americans. With our heads and fists held high, we asserted that "Black is Beautiful" to foster self-love and expression. We put on display natural hairstyles like braids, a detailed work of art of intricate lines and patterns extending from our crown. And afros that enveloped our faces and added an extra foot to one's height. We decorated our bodies with garments that honored our African heritage. Additionally, we rocked bright colors, crop tops and high-waisted or flared pants, platform shoes, and a bevy of suits – whether three pieces with peak lapels or double-breasted, made from corduroy, wool blends, or crushed velvet. We rejected mainstream media's representation of us as stereotypes and caricatures. Instead, creating defining art, entertainment, literature, and music that has captured our entire humanity.

Coming of age in the years following this era laid the foundation for who I am, giving me an innate passion for all things us – our history, perseverance, and beauty. My early influences taught me the importance of our worth as Black people and the value of loving ourselves, individually and as a community. In my eyes, we are fly, and our swagger is unmatched!

When I think about the contrast between how the two generations – parents and children – lived their lives, I'd say that Mama Opal and Daddy Matthew most certainly colored within the lines. Simultaneously, my mother stepped way outside of them. Take college, for instance. Mom went to Arizona State, partly because I was close by under my grandparents' care. It was also because Mama Opal did not want her daughter to attend the University of California, Berkeley. In my grandparents' minds, going to ASU– was to ensure that my mother stayed far away from the protest scene brewing in Berkeley. They knew Sonja would've been up there protesting and politicking. My mother already had a solid resolve to buck the system and change how things were being done. For her, as an academic, it was all about education and altering the plight of Black people. With her viewpoints, I think this may be why she gravitated toward the philosophies of the Black Panther Party.

The legacy of the Panthers is complicated. College students Huey Newton and Bobby Seale founded the collective in Oakland, California, in 1966 in response to police brutality against the Black community. But the Panthers are often misrepresented as a violent militant group who took up marching in the streets dressed in black berets and leather jackets, armed with .357 magnums, 12-gauge shotguns, and .45-caliber pistols. At the heart of the organization was a vision for Black unity and self defense, carried out through community survival programs and alliances with progressive whites and other groups of color. With a socialist-based ideology, the Panthers advocated for decent housing, employment, education, and freedom, among other demands. Their work included the creation of 35-plus initiatives to uplift the community, from legal aid, free medical clinics, establishing schools, and the noteworthy Free Breakfast for Children program.

I don't exactly know how my mother became a Black Panther. What I do know is that after graduating from ASU, she went back to California for work. I'm betting it was during that time she joined the organization. When I was four years old and joined her back in the Bay, I started school at Shelton's. The institution was a Black-owned preschool center with intimate class sizes of two teachers per two dozen children, and a curriculum that honored and taught African-American history. The following year, Mom placed me in kindergarten at an all-Black elementary school led by the Panthers. My recollection of that period is hazy. But what has stuck with me was being in the presence of Blackness every day. Here was an academic setting where the student-teacher ratio was small, something like ten-to-one. Children ate three home-cooked meals a day while at school. Most importantly, being taught by Black teachers provided students with a common language and a baseline of learning experiences. This is why the mission of the Panthers was so critical. For kids like me, we got to experience how powerful it was to be in an environment with Black educators who instilled pride and confidence within ourselves.

Being a student at that school opened my eyes to a whole other level of intellect. I'd never been in proximity to people showing up in Afrocentric ways. Compared to my first few years on the reservation, there wasn't a strong presence of the 'I'm Black, and I'm proud!' movement. It wasn't necessarily that my grandparents were not pro-Black. They just approached it differently. Mama Opal and Daddy Matthew were what I'd consider good middle-

SECOND ACT

class Black people. They weren't radical, but they contributed to the advancement of our community in the best way that they knew how. As educators, they could talk about the robust history of Black people that, to this day, is often left out of history books.

My mother, on the other hand, was overt in her approach. "You know, we must be ready for a revolution," she'd often say to me. Even though I was so young, that revolutionary energy, my mother's passion, became a part of my DNA. To this day, I still carry the confidence and fearlessness to advocate for the issues that matter most to our community and me.

I'm not sure how or when mom transitioned out of the party. I was only at that elementary school for a year before I started going to Kensington. I've never been clear on what Mom chose to pursue after leaving the Panthers. She traded one community – others may have perceived to be extreme – and joined another one that felt like a complete one-eighty for me.

***

As a Ph.D. candidate at UC Berkeley, Mom moved next door to Jehovah's Witnesses and interviewed them for her program. I can only guess if her dissertation had anything to do with religion. Still, something in her research became so paramount that she decided to convert.

When Mom chose to become a Witness, that was it. Everybody else had to acquiesce, including me. Any thoughts about celebrating birthdays and Christmases? That went out the window. At first, the idea of not commemorating those events like we used to made me scratch my head. But the effect of her choice was somewhat delayed on me since the rest of the family never changed how they engaged with me. Mama Opal and Daddy Matthew respected my mother's beliefs and new boundaries, but they were certainly bewildered. When I spent summers with them in Tyler, Texas, Mom found Witnesses I could accompany to the local Kingdom Hall, a Jehovah's Witnesses' place of worship. As two Southern Baptists who went to church on Sunday, my grandparents begrudgingly allowed me to attend the Hall. Over the holidays, though, they'd still slide me a couple of dollars, despite my mother insisting that they didn't buy me anything. I can hear Mama Opal and Daddy Matthew now, mumbling under their breath, "I don't know what you're talking about, lady." See, my grandparents were more like "good" southern folk. They avoided confrontation as much as possible but voiced their discontentment on the low, so the "chirren" couldn't hear.

In some ways, Mom became a much simpler person when she became a Witness. She toned down the bright and bold fashions. Mom also spoke less of revolution in exchange for living her life based on the Witnesses' interpretation of the Bible. If there's anything about my mother, when she commits herself to something, she puts her all into it.

Mom devoted herself to everyone around her, and many of the people she was serving in her ministry lived in government housing as we did. Forever the proud woman, for her, who we were as people was not defined by where we lived. She always told me, "What's going on outside this door is not what's happening inside this house." No matter where we were, Mom set up a home that always wrapped its presence around me like a hug. It was always our retreat, whether it was our first apartment with one bedroom, where she slept in the living room and I in the room, or our two-bedroom apartment in Crescent Park. In my mind, we weren't the typical Black people who lived in government housing. Instead, our place was a homage to her varied cultural experiences. She used to have 70s-style furniture, beaded curtains and bean bags, and the funky drum melody of Curtis Mayfield's "Superfly" seeping through the speakers filling the apartment. She had sand paintings and a customized rug from living on the reservation. My mother was the type who loved being surrounded by greenery. Plants filled our place and ivy grew all over. I had everything I wanted in my room – Mom accommodated me completely. Whereas she may have gotten her furniture from a second-hand store, mine was brand spanking new, like my day bed and bedroom set. I loved my white bed with the trundle underneath. Whenever I had anyone spend the night, I'd pull it out of its hiding place so my guest could sleep nearby.

As a Witness, a certain amount of respect was required in our house, even from guests. People had to act right when they came to Sonja's house. I didn't have many friends over because if they weren't Witnesses, she didn't allow me to have much company. Still, we had fun. We loved listening to music together. Enamored with Michael Jackson, Mom ensured I got all the albums and tickets to his concerts. She also bought me the Michael Jackson pins, "Beat It" jacket, and posters with his face were plastered all over my bedroom. As fans of all kinds of music, playing records at home was a ritual. New Edition was on rotation, as I'd walk around the apartment singing at the top of my lungs, "Candy Girl!

You are my world!" We'd sing and dance to the sounds of Bobby Caldwell, Gino Vanelli, and Christopher Cross. TV was also huge – Mom was a TV-holic! We had one in every room. That's how serious it was. She particularly loved Betty Davis movies. We'd snuggle up together under a blanket on the couch or in bed and watch old classics. I used to know almost every old movie. And whenever people came to our house, they'd stay for hours because mom would have on a good film.

Though she made some changes to her lifestyle, one thing that never changed was the vigor she had for debating. She wasn't going to let what she felt was an injustice skirt on by. She was not to be silenced, especially when it pertained to me. When I was seven or eight, I stood at five-eight, a height that, at the time, towered over the other kids at school. Though I was big in stature, I wasn't an aggressive child by any stretch of the imagination. I was mild for the most part and somewhat a tomboy. I was the person the boys always picked for their kickball or softball teams. In my class, a girl named Anna Jones used to always pick at me. I don't recall the exact circumstances, but on one day, in particular, I had had enough. She kept prodding the bear, and I snapped back at her. The next thing I knew, we were sent to the principal's office. Despite being the one who was bullied, the principal, Mr. Forsyth, threatened to suspend me from school.

Excuse me? Not Sonja Spigner's daughter.

After I called my mother and told her that Anna was bullying me and I was the one who faced a possible suspension, she marched herself up to my school. Mom was a single Black woman who lived in the flats. So you can imagine what this white man, at the helm of a white elementary school in the Hills in the early 70s, thought about this woman coming to defend her child. To him, there was no way Anna was bullying me because I was bigger than her.

"Since when does size dictate who's the aggressor here?" my mother demanded.

Though Mr. Forsyth continued to be kind of flippant with her, she held her ground.

"Let me help you understand something," she said, carefully articulating every word, like a slow build up in a song before the beat drops. "If Cheri is suspended, Anna needs to get suspended. If Anna is not suspended, Cheri better not be suspended. Or else the school board, the district, and the superintendent of Schools for the California Department of Education – will all have a letter from me."

Sonja was not one to be played with. I was her everything. But the matter also came down to principle. It was about what was fair. She refused to let this white man be prejudiced against her daughter because he assumed that this little white girl was never in the wrong. Still, I, the Black girl, had to be the aggressor based on my appearance and the community I lived in. Watching my mother taught me the significance of speaking up, whether it's against injustice in your neighborhood or workplace, or even expressing your needs and boundaries to the people around you. She gave me a baseline to emulate as I found my voice and advocated for myself in the corporate world years later.

I'll tell you one thing – after that, no one at school messed with me again. I can imagine the staff thinking, *'we do not want her momma coming up here!'*

After becoming a Witness, it felt like Mom got more protective of me. Sometimes I wonder if she had stayed with the Panthers longer, I might've had a bit more leeway since I would've probably spent most of my time with the other Panthers. Witnesses tend to go inward; while they live and work among the secular world, they still maintain a level of separation from it. As was her approach, Mom didn't do anything halfway. She became intensely focused on me and wanted me to do the right things, including not hanging out with the wrong types of children. Mom was always super protective of me. My mom had two boyfriends that I can remember, and she was mindful about bringing them around me. Otherwise, she didn't date a lot. As a Witness, you don't just date randomly; you date for marriage.

As a single parent, I'm sure Mom valued having a really good support system. As Witnesses, you get a tightly knit, built-in community. A very communal religion, they don't believe in you being with folks outside of it. These people are there to assist you in everyday life and in fulfilling your religious mission. Having a stable network because of the denomination is why it was partly challenging for me as I got older to reconcile that being a Witness wasn't the life I wanted. All my relationships in my late childhood, any skate events or slumber parties I attended, were with other Witnesses. When Mom went with a friend – also a Witness – to backpack around Europe, I was left behind and stayed with friends (yes, also Witnesses).

Looking back; it's funny to me how, even though Mom had a very structured lifestyle, she still did adventurous things. Being a Black woman in the early 80s, trekking from country to country like she did, was practically unheard of! Even though she went from coloring outside the lines to retreating within them, she was still radical in her own way by testing how far she could extend that line. Those are the kind of badass moments of my mom that I carry with me.

***

I was around six or seven when I realized that I wasn't like everybody else. I wasn't as bothered about it when I was around family, but subconsciously, I had this nagging feeling. Even though I was considered one of the cool kids despite being a Witness, I still went from doing what the rest of the kids in my class were doing to *not*. I wasn't allowed to participate in the same events and activities as they did, but I sure did try (I refused to be left out of Secret Santa!). Quite frankly, it was embarrassing—especially doing field service. Mom and I would go door-to-door, each holding a stack of pamphlets that read something like, *10 Questions & Answers on Jehovah's Witnesses. To make matters worse, we were* knocking on the doors of the families whose kids I was just in school with. If I could've made myself disappear in those moments, I would've. But from what I observed, other religions didn't require any unique behavior. I was the only one in my class who was a practicing Witness. And it wasn't enjoyable. Sometimes when you're growing up, you want to be part of the crowd. You don't want to stand out like a sore thumb, especially for something I had no control over.

Still, somewhere between 12 and 14, I got baptized. The procedure is unlike some churches, where everybody can go through it. To be a Witness, I had to study and answer questions before the baptism. I didn't go kicking and screaming, per se. To me, it was just an expectation that I had to fulfill. It felt like that was the thing to do, especially to be fully committed to something I was told I was part of. Not only that, the kids I considered my friends were getting baptized, and you don't always want to feel like an outcast.

Nevertheless, I couldn't shake that state of feeling ostracized from the community. Every religion has its flaws, and what I recognized was how judgmental people can be. The people at the Hall had a perception of me, that I was worldly and fast. Some parents didn't want their kids to hang around me; meanwhile, their kids were in all kinds of craziness! I don't know if it had something to do with my mom being a single parent because many Witnesses were married. Maybe it was because I was a very confident child. Mom used to buy me nice clothes, and I don't know if folks at the Hall felt as if I was upstaging them. I've long since learned that other folks' insecurities have everything to do with themselves and not me. But, as a pre-teen at the time, I couldn't shake the perception these people had of me. I used to ask and plead with Mom, "These people don't even like me. Why do you want to be around them? Why would you want to stay in this religion with these people who don't want their kids around me?"

***

Though my mother poured every ounce of herself and then some into me, something was still missing. She wasn't one to be overly emotional. She was the type who proved her love through actions, and not necessarily words or physical touch. Where she fell short in giving me hugs and accolades, my father more than made up for it. Quincey Newsome. That man was my cheerleader. If I'd told him I wanted to run for president, he would've said, "All right, let's do it! Whatever you need, Darlin'!" I could turn to my dad where my mom fell short in giving me the accolades I sought. My parents never got together after I was born, but I'll tell you one thing, Sonja got with a good one to give me what I needed.

Coming from a place where my mother was really strict, my father was the complete opposite. I always had more freedom with him. He was the life of the party! He was handsome, standing at 6'2" or 6'3" with a dimpled smile that could light up a room. He had a solid, somewhat athletic build with broad shoulders. His figure gave off the appearance that he worked out a bit, even though I never saw him at a gym once. But, I'm guessing his physique can be attributed to playing sports in his youth.

With strong negroid features, my dad had somewhat of a wide nose and full dark lips, which I credit to him smoking Kool cigarettes back in the day. His full beard was coarse, just like the hair on his head, though back in the 70s and 80s, he proudly had a Jheri Curl on display. From a distance, I could tell it was my daddy from his pimp walk, which today we call having that swag. When I went to Kensington, I was so excited to go to daddy-daughter night with him, looking all sharp amongst all those white parents! I loved his attitude towards life. With Quincey, it was about, "Hey, where's the party at? Where's the fun at?" He just took life by the horns and lived.

When I was young, while my mom left California to go to Arizona State, my dad went to college in Long Beach. While we grew to have a close relationship, the real credit for establishing the foundation for my dad and me to have a bond goes to Grandma Lillie. If it weren't for her, my dad could have been absent from my life. She was the glue, the one who provided stability and kept me and his side of the family super-duper connected. As a child, I was at Grandma Lillie's house almost every weekend, building tents out of blankets in the living room and playing tag outside with my cousins. I went to daddy's house every other weekend, which laid the foundation for me and his new wife, Sharon, to start having a relationship, especially when she had her own kids, my younger brothers, Quincey II and Sean. We all got close to the point where I was also a part of her family. I called her sister's aunties and her brother "Uncle Andre."

Daddy was nearly perfect in my eyes, but that didn't negate the fact that there were moments he disappointed me. There was a time when he was supposed to pick me up from my mom's. That day, she and I were sitting on the couch in the living room watching the Jerry Lewis Telethon, an annual charity broadcast. *Where is he?* I kept thinking, periodically peeking out the window to check on his arrival. Suddenly, I heard a familiar voice coming from the television. It was my dad on the telethon, giving away a check from his company! Mom and I looked on in shock. My dad. The same person who was supposed to knock on the door at any moment to pick me up. We still couldn't believe it was him. But it was him, for sure. The light was shining, and he would be in it, no matter his commitment to his daughter. He was an only child like me, and sometimes, it was difficult for him to think about others. But as I grew older, I understood the challenges he was battling.

Sonja chose Jehovah, but Quincey was the opposite. My daddy was a streets man, and that's the religion he followed for a long time.

SECOND ACT

Daddy was always out there – smoking, drinking, doing drugs. And he certainly couldn't keep his eyes or hands off the women. I didn't exactly notice it until he and Sharon got a divorce. After that, he always had a different girlfriend, some of whom he lived with. I knew first-hand because, more than once, I'd get pulled into the drama. Women would threaten to kick my dad out of their home and back onto the streets. Some of them told me directly. One time I was at home, and the phone rang off the hook.

"Hello?"

"...is this Cheri? Quincey's daughter?"

I asked who was calling. The voice on the other end was a woman. She told me her name was Francine and that she was seeing my dad.

Why is she calling me?

I didn't have to wait much longer to find out.

"You need to come get your daddy because I'ma put him out!" She said before slamming down the phone.

No way I was going to let my dad sleep on the street. Jumping into my Toyota Camry, I drove across town until I found him standing at the end of Francine's driveway with a single duffle bag thrown over his shoulder. When I pulled up beside him, he opened the passenger door and sank into the seat. The man sitting next to me was unlike the one I knew. This wasn't the lively, self-assured person who, if you looked up the definition of swag in the dictionary, his picture would be next to it. Fidgeting his body and avoiding my eyes, I could tell he was ashamed. His daughter had to come and save him. My father was a proud man, and this was not one of his finest moments. I was present and showed up as his alibi more times than I can count. It set a precedent for how I'd approach my relationship with men in the future. Observing how he treated women had such an impact on the people I chose to date later on. His behavior, particularly the infidelity, turned into something I'd become comfortable with.

Throughout high school, my dad continued to struggle with his drug addiction. At one point, after he and my stepmother broke up, he needed a place to go. I begged my mom to let him stay with us. As disappointed as I was with him, my first instinct was to give him the love and support he so desperately needed. Thankfully, it didn't take much to convince her. We made space for Dad in the living room to sleep. Seeing what he was going through, this man, whom I looked at as my hero, was disappointing. When everything else in my life was super stable, he was the one factor that wasn't. Since he reached a point in his life where there was nowhere to go, but up, I felt like I had earned the right to say how I felt. I needed to get out all those years of being let down and never really saying anything. The roles, in this case, were reversed – I was the adult instead of the child. He needed to assess where he was and evaluate the steps that got him there so he could pivot. He needed some stability in his life. Choosing my words delicately, I expressed my love for him, and how I didn't enjoy seeing him in his state.

Even when it's our parents, those honest conversations have to happen. We can still honor them and speak with respect. Because

SECOND ACT

I knew this person sleeping in my living room wasn't who my dad was. He didn't say much but acknowledged that he was listening. I'd hoped he felt like I was a safe space for him, and I think I managed to do that. He didn't hide his vulnerability, gripping me close in his embrace as he apologized. I'd learn this years later, but even back then, I could separate my dad from what he did and still love him for him.

Regardless of his flaws, that was my guy. When I began stepping out and getting into my own predicaments, the one thing he never did was judge me. He always had my back. I'd be out drinking and hanging out with the wrong people, and there were plenty of times he would pick me up from some crazy situations. Things neither he nor I ever told my mother. I explored things I had no business doing, hanging out with people doing drugs and heroin. But I'd call him, pleading into the phone, "Daddy, you gotta come get me." And he'd come without hesitation. Since my dad was also raised in a strict religious household, I think that really made us in sync. Grandma Lillie and her sisters were Holiness, speaking in tongues, being in church all day, not listening to secular music type of folk. At a young age, my dad started rebelling and went out into the world to do what he wanted. He used to tell me, "If it makes you feel good, do it." He was one of the first people I ever heard say, "If you like it, I love it, Darlin'." That's not to say he wouldn't voice his opinion or tell me what he thought. Nonetheless, he would still ride with me. With my dad, I got the safe space that I needed, a contrast from when things came to a head at home with my mother.

***

To prepare for the world, I was groomed to be proud, confident, and fearless. But at home, my wings folded tight at my side like a bird as I abided by the restrictions my mother set.

As my high school ended, I knew my next step was college. I was set to graduate in the spring of 1988. All my life, the importance of education – from Mama Opal, Daddy Matthew, and my mother – was drilled into my head. I applied to several colleges and got accepted into most of them, including Howard University and UCLA. I was already envisioning what my life as a college student was going to be like. I planned to major in communications (Oprah was the inspiration). And just like I saw when I went to Arizona State with my mom, I'd walk across the campus with my books in hand, letting out a gut-busting laugh with my friends as we headed to class.

When the time came, I couldn't wait to share the news with my mom. it was a huge accomplishment for me to go to a prestigious college. It's what she trained me for and what I worked so hard to achieve. I was going to tell everyone I knew. All my friends were heading off to school, too, and that's all we could talk about. Along with my acceptance, I was required to fill out my financial aid paperwork to apply for housing. One evening I approached my mom in the living room. My excitement overflowed as I asked her to review and sign the form. I just knew she would share my elation, and I could already see her telling me how proud she was of me.

Instead, I was completely blindsided by her response.

She declined to sign the papers.

SECOND ACT

"You don't need to do that," she said dryly. "You just need to stay here and study."

One of my mother's strongest attributes was her dedication to causes she believed in. But her faith was steadily creating a significant rift between us – and this was the tipping point. Witnesses discouraged investing in higher education in those days as they believed the world was ending soon. And that's what she abided by. My whole life revolved around education. But my heart sank in my chest to have my mother, a woman with two degrees and a partial doctorate, tell me I didn't need college. It was as if someone had dropped a glass vase on purpose and shattered my dream into pieces.

"You're not going to help me?" I pleaded with her. I couldn't believe that she would rob me of this opportunity. All I needed was her tax returns for the paperwork, but she wasn't having it.

I never saw it coming. And I couldn't hold my tongue any longer. A sense of betrayal rushed over my body, and I lashed out at her. I shouted that I felt controlled by a religion I didn't choose, and now it was standing between me and my goals. I told her that I was a good person, and I knew God saw that. So how could she do this? As much as I loved my mother, in that moment, I was hurt and frustrated by her decision not to support me.

CHAPTER 3

Grown Woman

The teenage years are a difficult phase. We're dealing with awkward changes to our bodies and longing for a peer group to attach ourselves to. All the while trying to discover who we are without the influence of our momma, daddy, grandparents, or whoever else. And then there comes the point when some young adults think they got it all together. That was me. I thought I was grown, honey, okay? I was pushing boundaries and feeling myself, flexing my independence to the fullest. At times, I found myself in some very sticky adult situations – all of which stemmed from my curiosity to explore the world outside of the confines of my strict religious household.

Having the 80s as the backdrop for my coming-of-age period was certainly interesting. But beyond my front door, Oakland was changing. And not for the better. The drugs that infiltrated our community brought us to our knees. Just as they did in every other major Black city across the country, addiction and violence ran rampant. People you used to know around the way – neighbors, veterans of the Vietnam War, or even family members – became regulars on the streets. Some were walking around in a perpetual daze with no sign of life in their eyes. Folks looking for their next hit would crowd dozens of street corners as if lining up at the unemployment office, but instead, it was where cocaine and heroin could be bought day or night. I remember there was one part of town called 69 Village. People would usually get off the BART bus and walk over there to pick up their drugs.

Being an adolescent in those days made all of us grow up instantly. The young boys who used to pass the time playing baseball, football, and dodgeball in the street turned into corner lookouts. The 10-year-old kid that used to be a regular at the Eastshore Community Center in Richmond, or the Rainbow Center in Oakland traded that in for a job packing clouds of white powder in plastic baggies, prepping them for the next eager customer. Oakland was the town of many drug dealers, particularly legends like Lil D, and the infamous kingpin Felix Wayne Mitchell Jr. (the inspiration for the movie *New Jack City*). Known as "Felix The Cat," he created what many say is the country's first large-scale operation, extending from California all the way to the Midwest. As pre-teens and teenagers, we saw how drugs ravished our community. But we also noticed another side to it - flashy wealth. These kingpins became Oakland's version of Black billionaires, as it was common to see them rolling through the streets in Bentleys and Rolls Royces, flaunting heavy gold chains around their necks and other gaudy jewelry, mink coats, and of course, beautiful women. As a kid, whether you came from a poverty-stricken home or a household where you saw your parents working two or more jobs living paycheck to paycheck, seeing what was happening on the streets was fascinating. By joining one of the drug organizations, a young boy could start as a cop spotter on the corner. He could make a couple of hundred dollars a week, and then rise through the ranks to become a distributor and pull in thousands.

Between the drugs and the competition between dealers, daily violence escalated significantly. The headlines plastered on newspapers like the Oakland Tribune were about two things—crack and drive-by shootings, as rivals would constantly cruise around and unload on each other. People were afraid to leave their homes after dark for fear of getting hit by a stray bullet. I was witnessing all of this from the sidelines. Those of us teens who weren't participating in that lifestyle couldn't go to those typical social outings like the movies. So, leaving my neighborhood gave me a sense of relief. Whenever I visited a friend, I could let my guard down and simply enjoy myself. But once I stepped foot back in Crescent Park, my instincts kicked in, and I knew that at any time, I'd have to hit the deck when the blast of a bullet was released into the air.

Though I knew some people who engaged in that life of hustle, drugs, and violence, Mom was very clear on what she was and was not going to allow. "You see that," she said to me once, pointing in the direction of our apartment window. She was focusing on the boys in the distance, standing idly on the corner until someone approached them to make an exchange. "In here, we have what we're gonna do, and that…" she emphasized, drawing my attention to the random tweaker outside, "…is what we're not gonna do."

There was no guessing with mom. She was pretty cut and dry and black and white about what we did or did not do, especially as Witnesses. Still, it didn't hold me back from stepping outside the safety bubble that she built for me.

SECOND ACT

I started middle school in 1982, where my peer group turned into the earliest sign of the evolution I was going through. My social factions collided, and I no longer felt like I was in two different spaces. The kids that went to Kensington with my friends and me from the neighborhood – I now saw all of them in the same place. I had classes with my white friends, but I could hang out with my friends from Crescent Park, Kennedy Manor, and the other housing communities in the area before school, on the bus, at lunch, and after school. Before, I always felt like I had to associate with Witnesses. But now, I had the luxury of connecting with whomever I wanted to. And I was cool with everyone.

By the time I got to high school, my social circle had expanded with folks involved in the drug game. During that time, I was getting my education from the books and the classroom, but with such a voracious curiosity, the streets turned into another teacher. Though I was inquisitive, my naivete had me in some suspect places. I've actually been at a table where a young woman I knew, her name was Corey, was smoking rock cocaine, and I had no idea what it was. Or the time when, unbeknownst to me, I was dating one of the biggest drug dealers in Oakland but had no idea who he was. There I was with my bubbly self, asking this guy if he liked Prince or Michael Jackson. Imagine my surprise when I found out who he was. Yes, I felt foolish.

The funny thing is, stuff was always going on around me, but somehow, I was always protected. There were times I'd literally leave someone's apartment, and not long after, someone there got shot or arrested. There were many moments when I felt like God was watching over me.

And so was my dad.

A lot of my sticky moments came from the boyfriends I had. One of them, Seth, used to hang out with a guy who was a pimp and a drug dealer. And I would be right there, hanging out with the girls his friend was pimping. Back then, and still, to this day, I don't have a lot of judgment about people and what they do. I liked those girls, and I befriended one of them. Honestly, those sex workers were so interesting to me. I was lowkey impressed, like, *shoot—there's a bunch of people having sex for free. At least you get paid!* My rationale was that they had free will. Since I grew up in a rather strict and protected environment, I found aspects of those women's childhoods intriguing. Looking back, I was always trying to empower those women, even if it wasn't the best advice to be dishing out in those surroundings.

"Girl, you know you don't have to do this!" I'd say to them. "You could do something else instead and be getting your own money!" Clearly, my naivety was showing because Lord knows I could've gotten them in trouble talking to them that way.

What I also didn't know was that Seth had a heroin addiction. I found out when a group of us were at his house getting ready to go out. I was the last to know. Seth's friends liked me and felt that I was good for him. Which is why they didn't want me to find out he was using and stop dating him. I was still a liability that could've messed up what they had going on. Still, my mom did her job putting the fear of God in me about drugs. When I finally learned the truth about Seth, my inner alarm went off. *Hmm, I don't know about this.*

That's when I picked up the phone to call my dad.

With my dad, I could always depend on him to pick me up from some shady situations. Once, I went to an event at school and had way too much to drink. I wasn't a heavy drinker then, and I'm still not today. But I was drunk, and of course, couldn't drive home. So, I asked my dad to pick me up.

"You know you can't go home to your mama's house right now, right?" he'd say.

"Yessss," I slurred, looking at him with a sly grin on my face.

He'd let out a chuckle in that, *I know the game*, type of way, from one player to another. "Let me call your mama and tell her you're coming to my house," he'd say. There were plenty of times he'd call my mom on my behalf and tell her, "I'll pick Cheri up and take her with me over to my house." As far as I'm aware, daddy kept our secrets between us, away from my mother's knowledge.

I'm pretty sure my dad knew my mom was super strict. Despite all my risky adventures, I think he knew I was smart and, ultimately, I would make the right decision. It was unspoken, but we connected over growing up in restrictive households, him from his upbringing with Grandma Lillie being Holiness. I'm sure he just concluded that there was no reason to try and be overbearing with me. He wouldn't let me completely off the hook, though, because he was still going to voice his perspective as someone who knew the ins and outs of street life. "We'll talk about it later," was his thing. Ultimately, I think he knew I had a good head on my shoulders, and in some ways, he saw himself in me.

***

While it can be challenging for some, for me, high school was where it was at! Even though I couldn't do all the stuff like go to prom because Mom wouldn't let me, that didn't stop my fun. I started feeling myself differently, like I was coming into my own. And once I tasted freedom, I couldn't let up.

Since my school district stopped bussing in the mid-70s, I'd catch the Alameda County (AC) transit bus. Because of that, I could cut school and do what I wanted because nobody knew where I was. And once Daddy Matthew and Mama Opal bought me a Hyundai Excel my junior year, let me tell you, it was a wrap! I was already accepted into college during my junior year, so I knew which classes I had to attend to graduate. I only needed three courses to pass. So, my strategy was to schedule those classes around the same period, sequentially, like second and third or third or fourth. Then I was out for the rest of the day. Mom had no idea.

High school was also a time when I was drawn to bad boys. Why do good girls like bad guys? It's a question as old as time. The typical explanation is that women are attracted to bad boys because there's some type of protection there. While there is some validity to this, for me, the thing about bad boys was that I could always see some good in them. No matter how rugged of an exterior someone had. Many people today perceive me as very feminine, and even back then, I think that side of me was always able to draw out the sweeter side of those young men. I believe some of that had to do with, subconsciously, wanting to be in direct contrast to my mother. She wasn't shy about judging people for who or what they did. Seeing that, I'm sure, had something to do with my being intentional that I didn't act the same towards people.

By some women's standards, my dad could've been considered a bad boy, a womanizer and a drug abuser. But to me, my dad was cool. Yes, he was a street guy but I wouldn't classify him as a bad boy, per se. He had swag dripping all over. He dressed well. He wasn't the smartest guy, but he was a good person. And he was my first lesson in helping me see beyond people's baggage – because we've all got something no matter who it is.

If I were to pinpoint my attraction to bad boys, I'd say I was also intrigued by seeing people, like my dad, living on the edge a little bit. There was excitement to it. And when I think back, perhaps I was in a space where there were aspects of my personality that I wanted to satisfy. And when I say that, I mean take chances, and push the envelope a little bit. Mom was notorious for saying, "Girl, don't be doing that." She was so protective, and it had a lot to do with my need to expand my freedom. *"Don't do that. You gon' get hurt."* I was all about trying to move outside of those safety nets. What's living if you can't live a little? I wanted the autonomy to figure myself out without having anyone put expectations on me.

Linking up with these bad boys, I was a ride or die – to a point. I had boundaries, for sure. I wouldn't go too far out on a limb, but the moments I did, were pretty eventful. When I was dating that guy who was one of the biggest drug dealers in Oakland, his brother was a fugitive at the time. I had no idea. To me, he was so sweet. I'd do things like grocery shop for him and take him on outings to get him out of the house. I'd even bring some of my friends to hang out with him. (My boyfriend, and I use that label loosely, wasn't around because he and his brother couldn't get caught together.) Essentially, I'd play messenger for the brother, communicating on his behalf to other people. Then one day, I saw the news and found out that the brother was a person of interest. "Oh my God!" I shrieked. Not only was I in shock, but I was also confused. I questioned my ability to assess people's character, wondering how I could be so close to a fugitive and not even know it. "Oh no, this is just too much," I said, shaking my head in disbelief as I reached for the phone. This "big killer," who was like my big brother, was on the run and got caught in another state. I had to call some friends to confirm what I had just seen on TV was real.

I won't lie – some perks came from being with these types of guys. There was money abound, so you could always have the finer things. I have expensive taste, and I can thank my mom for that! She always brought me nice things, which I became accustomed to. These hustlers and drug dealers weren't on the straight and narrow path, of course, but as a teenager, being with someone I was free to be myself around and who wouldn't hesitate to spoil me made me feel appreciated.

Even though I had boyfriends, I wasn't officially allowed to date. There was no discussion about it, either. It wasn't an option. As a Witness, you were only allowed to date for marriage, and I couldn't date anyone who wasn't a Witness. If none of those options were on the table, forget it. I used to go skating with one of my best friends and a broader group of teens who were Witnesses. People were always coupled up. It was kind of outside of the parents' purview. I don't know if the parents looked the other way or actually thought we were all sweet and innocent.

SECOND ACT

Sex was not a topic to be discussed, either. It was that you simply, didn't have it until you got married. I think mothers like mine believe they are trying to protect their children by avoiding discussions about relationships and sex. But, it, in fact, leaves us more vulnerable. It leaves us unprepared and lacking the tools to know what a healthy sexual or romantic relationship should look like. This silence can be costly. It further spreads the notion that talking about sex is taboo and leaves people feeling uncomfortable with their bodies and the sexual experiences they may have with others.

I didn't have much conversation with other people about sex. Some of the Witness girls were having sex, contrary to what their parents thought, and they would tell the rest of us about it. At that point, all the sex talk was about penetration. No intimacy. It was just this act. No one described what good sex should be like. During that era, almost everyone watched the 1982 movie *Fast Times at Ridgemont High*, about a group of high school students experimenting with drugs and sex. Unfortunately, watching that movie, and other sex scenes, never illustrated sex as pleasurable. Even porn back in those days wasn't about pleasure.

In spite of my lack of knowledge about sex, I had no hang-ups or insecurities regarding my body image. I went through a bit of an awkward stage, but overall, mom and dad raised me to have an overflow of confidence. I wasn't influenced by media images or other girls at school. I was tall from childhood, so I had a long time to get used to being bigger than everyone else. In elementary school, I was probably 5'8 (today, I'm 5'9 and ¼). But Mom always reminded me, *shoulders back, chin up*. Her perspective was, if you're going to be tall, proudly own it! She always dressed me well, ensuring that I had all the latest fashions that were hot back then – Guess jeans, Sassoon dresses, and Calvin Klein suits. It helped to build my confidence (and affinity for the finer things in life).

One of the problems I had as a tall young woman was having to wear a size ten shoe. Since nobody made girl shoes in that size then, (unless they were heels, which I was too young to wear), Mom had to get mine from overseas. She found a shop in San Francisco that got shoes shipped directly from Europe. The shoes she bought for me would be flat and expensive, made of leather, and from Italy. I was the best dressed in high school with my shoes and Jordache jeans! But by the time my age caught up with my body, I was quite secure.

Between junior and senior year, at 17, I lost my virginity. The fallout from it went completely against Mom's rulebook. My doctor's secretary was a Witness. Since she had access to my files, she found out I was sexually active. Instead of keeping it to herself, she shared the news with my doctor and then spread the gossip to the elders around the Hall. As a Witness, she felt obligated to tell that I had this 'secret' that was against the principles of the religion. With the news out there, it led to my disfellowship from the congregation. Despite my animosity for the religion, being disfellowshipped as a teenager was still hard. I was young enough to still live at home, so I had to continue attending meetings with Mom. Except I wasn't allowed to talk or interact with anyone. No doubt, Mom was disappointed. But like so many other things, there wasn't much discussion about it.

***

SECOND ACT

The bombshell about my mom's decision to forgo helping me with college completely derailed the plan I thought I was going to follow. When the news reached my grandparents, they exploded. At 18 years old, it was the first time I ever heard Daddy Matthew curse at my mom. He and Mama Opal were all about education and ensured that mom got one without ever having to pay for it. They were flabbergasted by her choice.

"This is going too far!" Daddy Matthew snapped. "This religion is going too far!"

But she wasn't budging. However, my grandparents were willing to pay for me to attend school. But it turned out there was some paperwork I needed to have that got all screwed up in the process.

College was on hold. And it left me with, what I felt, was no other choice. I thought, *Oh well, I'll just do what I want to do*. It was time to assert my independence. After graduating high school, in the summer of 1989, I moved out. Of course, Mom wasn't happy about my choice. After leaving home, I stayed with my aunt for a period, and another time with some friends, until I found my own place. I ended up getting a two-bedroom apartment with my friend Bobbi at the Hilltop Bayview apartment complex. I may have felt grown before, but now, I was fully autonomous.

One day, as Bobbi and I were walking through the lobby of our complex, we passed by a security guard who caught my attention. He was handsome, and I could tell he had an athletic build. As Bobbi and I walked away from the security booth, his eyes connected with mine. *It's gonna be fun living here*, I thought. We both looked at each other, giving the unspoken, *Okay, I see you*. He stopped us before we were out of range and introduced himself. His name was Tommy.

For weeks, whenever I'd leave or come into the complex and he was working, he'd stop and strike up a conversation with me. It turns out, he was 28. But it didn't bother me at all. I knew I had it going on. I had my own apartment, my own car, and a full-time job at Wells Fargo in the customer service department. And now here was this man, this older gentleman with his own job, flirting with me. I don't recall who asked who out first, but one day, he called my apartment. Bobbi answered, and a few seconds later, I heard her yell, "Cheri, it's the security guard!"

Tommy was the first guy to date me. Those boyfriends I had in the past, we hung out, but Tommy and I would run errands, go to the movies, or have dinner together. We were actually dating, and I liked that. A few months in, Tommy asked me if he could come back to my place, and I let him. At that time, I was still sleeping on my day bed that I brought with me from Mom's house since I didn't have money to buy too much new furniture. When he came over that night, it was the first time we had sex.

Although I had sex before, I wasn't promiscuous about it. With Tommy, I wasn't just having sex and it wasn't only about penetration either. I was experiencing intimacy and sensuality. He gently kissed me, on my lips, on my neck, and made his way down my body, kissing me all over in places I never thought could feel so gratifying. He took his time, being gentle and tender. With our aroused bodies intertwined, he'd caress my back and my thighs,

SECOND ACT

and cup my breasts in his hands. And that was the first time I climaxed.

I hadn't known what an orgasm was until Tommy. *So, this is what it's like*, I thought. From that euphoric moment, I became hooked on him.

CHAPTER 4

Through the Storm

Tommy came along at a time that coincided with my new-found freedom as a young adult. I was making my own money, reveling in the newness of it all. I was living on my own and could stay out late without having to return home and answer to my mother. I also had a man I was dating who could visit and spend the night at my apartment. Without any restrictions, I could have a boyfriend in a different way than I had before. It was unlike the boyfriends I had in the past, when we'd pass the time just kicking it at their house or a friend's house. It was my first seemingly mature relationship with a grown man.

Except neither one of us was equipped with the skills to handle it.

During that time, no one in our community conversed about proper courting and what that looked like. Parents were too busy making certain that we - as teenagers - weren't having sex that they completely forgot about giving us the tools to have proper relationships. Trying to protect me, Mom never openly discussed relationships, men, or sex with me. As a result, I had no preparation for having a healthy relationship, period, let alone one as extreme as mine and Tommy's. Despite his rich, dark caramel skin, light brown eyes, muscular physique and sense of humor, Tommy was broken. When a relationship becomes toxic and unhealthy, we often see the red flags early on but dismiss them. With Tommy, there were warning signs everywhere. Yet how would I have known? Being young and having, what I thought at the time, was bomb sex, it was pretty easy to become infatuated with someone without serious thought about who they are as a person.

Being compatible versus having chemistry are two different things, and I'd learn that years later. When you're 18, 19, or 20-years-old, you're not making decisions about relationships based on core values, building a legacy, or walking in your purpose. The most conflict between people in relationships comes from a lack of communication and doing our due diligence. Questions like, *what do you value? Where do you see yourself?* These are indications of the type of person you're dealing with. It's about choosing someone based on character versus attraction or those surface-level things that we instantly latch on to. Even to this day, I still don't know what Tommy's core values are. From the start, I wasn't asking the right questions. I didn't vet him properly. And his motivations for entering a relationship with me were ill-placed, too. As an older man, I think he was attracted to someone who hadn't grown into herself yet. For me, in some ways, my fixation with him was about my need to get away from my mother.

Tommy was no good right from the start, but I was already too deep in it to realize it. When I talk about being ride or die, that was me in those early days. Looking back, I don't know if I entirely felt emotionally safe with him. Our connection was a 'me and you against the world' dynamic. I put the relationship before me because, for the first time, I had a man who claimed me as his woman. I was a bit caught up in the fantasy of us being boyfriend and girlfriend. And so, when people told me he was not good for me, I dug in to prove they were wrong because I didn't want to concede that they were right. Still, it wasn't as if those warning signs were hidden and tucked far away for me to notice. They were glaring in my face, practically screaming, and waving their hands to snap my oblivious self out of the made-up world I was in.

The first red flag: he was still living with his mama.

The second: his jealousy.

Third: his children.

By the time Tommy and I got together, he'd already had two children, with one on the way. He didn't tell me at first. Once he did, that could've been my opportunity to bow out and leave that man alone. But I didn't. I felt I had some allegiance and loyalty to him, especially when it came to the woman carrying his third child. When she was pregnant and trying to get child support from him, there I was fanning the flames.

"We ain't going to be giving her no child support!" I declared.

Life has a way of dishing out irony. Unbeknownst to me, I'd become that woman soon enough, wanting Tommy to live up to his responsibilities as a father.

Despite overlooking all the ominous signals, I was adamant about not wanting to be with a man who didn't show up for his children. I didn't encourage him to be an absentee father (though there were already indications of that, too). One weekend, in January 1990, he and I went to pick up his oldest daughter to come and stay with us. Over those two days we had her, she gravitated towards me. Intensely. She'd follow me around my apartment, cuddling up next to me when we sat on the couch. Whenever I stood at the sink to wash dishes, she gripped her delicate arms around my leg.

That's odd, I thought. Then trying to figure out why she was clinging to me, it finally hit me.

I wonder if I'm pregnant.

Sure enough, I was.

Since Tommy and I weren't married when I got pregnant, I was a bit fearful of telling my mom. I had no idea what she was going to say about the situation. I knew she wasn't fond of Tommy, not in the least. Parents can read people, and my mom knew he wasn't the one. Once I finally worked up the nerve to tell her, she gave me her standard, practical response.

"Okay, so daycare is expensive. How are you going to do that?" She asked.

And since her religion was still important to her, she also dropped the 'M' word on me. "Are you guys thinking about or talking about getting married?"

In July 1991, ten months after our first daughter, Julian, was born, Tommy and I hopped into my car and drove three and a half hours to Reno to get married. There was no surprise or romantic proposal. No getting down on one knee. No declaration of his love for our young family or me. There we were, standing at the justice of the peace in our street clothes. Me, in a FILA jacket with some Sassoon or Guess jeans and EBS tennis shoes on my feet. Tommy wore something similar.

This marriage was doomed from the beginning. Long before we ever drove to Reno, the relationship became abusive. People stay for different reasons when it comes to matters of the heart. As women, especially Black women, we tend to fall into the role of martyrs, heavily resting the weight of the world on our shoulders and backs. We don't want to fail, even when everything tells us something isn't working. I think for Tommy, what drove his decision to become legally bound to me was a sense of urgency, as in, *if I don't do this, she's probably not going to be with me.* But really, I think it was a control tactic. For me, I agreed to marry him so I wouldn't become a single parent, a title I never asked for. I wanted better for myself than to raise my baby alone, and carry the stigma that sometimes comes with being a single mother.

Tommy and I had many battles. He could be extremely jealous and cruel, and I wasn't prepared to deal with that. However, I was no shrinking violet by any means. I still came up in the hood. I wouldn't back down from an argument or fight with him. While he didn't treat me the way I should've been treated, I also didn't have the tools to be constructive in how I responded to him. Our fights were vulgar and vicious. I don't remember all of them, but they were nasty. If there was anything Tommy could be jealous about, he'd find it. When I was six or seven months pregnant with Julian, he and I were walking around at the mall when I bumped into someone I went to high school with. Since we hadn't seen each other in a while, we expressed our pleasant surprise at seeing one another, swiftly updating each other on our lives since graduation. He hugged me, and that was that.

When Tommy and I got home, he exploded. He asked me if I was pregnant by the guy and alleged that I had cheated. *Whoa, what's going on right now?* I thought. Conversely, there were many times when I was destructive, too. Instead of dealing with my issues, I'd instigate a conflict. I wanted him to be as frustrated as I was. I would get angry at seemingly one thing, when in actuality, I was angry he had three kids before I even knew it. I would say something to trigger him because I was mad I was in this relationship. I knew the exact buttons to push to get him upset. One of them was his insecurity about his deferred dream of playing professional football. As with many young, urban men, sports are their ticket to getting out of the hood. Tommy was no different in that way. In college, he was a popular defensive back. But in his junior year, Tommy broke his neck while tackling someone on the opposite team. That just snatched away everything he thought he would have, and I don't know if he ever recovered from it.

Back then, when you broke your neck, you'd have to wear one of those halo rings, with adjustable metal bars attached to a vest that fits around your chest and a metal "ring" fixated around your head. Because of that, Tommy was super sensitive about the halo ring's indentations left on his forehead. I would say something about that when I was trying to get him upset. Knowing that was a physical insecurity, I'd exploit it. And he knew which attribute of mine to call out. Therefore, when he talked about me, he'd point out my chin whiskers (which I've long since had removed).

"Oh, so you must be a man," he'd spew at me.

"Then you must be gay," I snapped back.

We'd just be talking about each other badly, in all kinds of ways. In some ways, I wonder if that was a response to my need to express myself after so many years of not being able to express myself the way I wanted. At my core, I didn't trust him. Not with my heart. When you're conflicted, everything's an argument. Everything is a problem, or it can be, even if it's something that may or may not have been. All because the relationship is built on the wrong foundation.

The brawls Tommy and I had were just as physical as they were verbal. One time, we were in the car and got into an argument. As I was driving, he punched me in the face. With streams of crimson trickling down my face, I pulled over and kicked him out of the car. When Julian was a baby, there was a time when I went to work with deep tones of blue and purple under my right eye. I lied to my co-worker, telling her my daughter kicked me in the face. (I felt that was a plausible story since Julian wore walking shoes with hard soles back then.) That was one of many lies I told people.

While all of this was happening, I became withdrawn from most of my family and friends. I didn't speak a word about the stuff that was happening, even though people around me saw it. Frankly, I was embarrassed. But my parents knew. And they pleaded with me to leave. One time, my mom had to pick me up from my apartment in the middle of the night and take me to the hospital. I needed stitches for my eye after Tommy assaulted me. There was another incident when Tommy had an apartment in Oakland.

SECOND ACT

While there, I found a picture of him at the Berkeley Marina with his ex when she was in town. I noticed he had on clothes I recently bought him, indicating that this meeting happened while we were together. And he never told me about it.

I can't say for sure whether Tommy slept with someone else while we were a couple. But I knew he could be inappropriate with women, and lying was not something I tolerated. Confronting him about the picture, Tommy tried to tell me there was nothing to be suspicious of since the meet-up happened long ago. Now, I'm smarter than the average bear, so in this case, when he told me he was at a place at a particular time, I started calculating and adding things up. If there is anything that infuriates me, it's when people lie and try to insult my intelligence.

"No, this wasn't when you said it was," I retorted, my blood pressure rising. "You're wearing the sweater that I bought you!"

As he continued denying it, I walked over to the kitchen and grabbed a glass out of the cabinet. I broke it against the counter and went to lunge at him. Amid trying to attack him, I felt the glass make a sharp slash on my arm, spurts of blood erupting from the open cut. The police were called, and I was taken to the hospital. At the time, people who tried to commit suicide were kept there (I wasn't trying to commit suicide, but I'd rather have been taken there instead of jail for attempting to kill Tommy). My parents met me at the hospital and never left my side. They suffered with me during those couple of years I was with Tommy. And it wore on them a lot. What they were seeing was so different from anything they envisioned for me.

61

Between Tommy and me, our exchanges were beyond anything I had been exposed to or experienced. Mom pretty much sheltered me, and Daddy Matthew and Mama Opal had a perfect marriage in my eyes. With my dad and stepmother, I was at their house every other weekend, and I think they put their best foot forward when I was there. From Tommy's perspective, this was learned behavior. He witnessed abuse from his parents and didn't have good coping skills. His aggression was how he expressed his emotions. Nobody taught him how to navigate conflict in relationships; many Black men of the pre-millennial generation do not get help for emotional, physical, and mental trauma.

I think about how I brought elements of my mom into my relationship and marriage. Mainly, her need to debate, be right, and not let things go. It's one thing to have an intellectual debate. However, in a relationship, where there's a lot of feelings, passion, and all kinds of emotions mixed in, that's when it can potentially become toxic. I hadn't learned nor had any skills around that type of conflict resolution because I'd never felt that way about someone before. All these emotions and experiences were so foreign to me. It caught me off guard, and I didn't know how to handle it. Tommy wasn't like my dad or Daddy Matthew, so I wasn't naturally inclined to mirror Mama Opal's behavior as a wife. As I've gotten older, I've learned that as women, we will follow a man who leads in his strength. Tommy wasn't a leader. He went from his mother's house to living with me. He wasn't the provider. My mom was such a strong person, and though she never said it, she exuded that "I don't need a man" type of energy. I don't recall ever saying anything like that, but I wouldn't be surprised if I made Tommy feel emasculated. Ultimately, I was probably bigger than what he was. Yet, I think I felt less dominant because he was seven years older than me.

What Tommy and I had was never love – it was lust. But I stayed in that relationship long past its expiration date because I didn't want to be a single mother. It's not something I resent him for because it was my choice. Looking back on those tumultuous two years, I've asked myself what else was behind my decision to stay. *Was I trying to keep him by any means? Did I not want to fail?* That's part of it. It was my first marriage. I didn't take rejection well and needed to succeed at all costs. In my mind, I needed to win.

I'm going to show him how to love me.

I'm going to show him my worth.

I'm going to show him my value.

Regardless of what I thought, I didn't have the power to change him. Ultimately, I would never be suitable for him because a great woman is never good enough for the wrong man, no matter how hard she tries. As women, more of us need to take responsibility for our resolve to do that. To this day, I see Tommy as a victim. He is wounded and still hasn't figured his life out. I see him as not taking accountability for his wrongs and his role in our relationship. Instead, he's always found a way to blame others. That lack of responsibility has kept him small and stagnant some three decades later.

For anyone coming from an abusive relationship, it doesn't have to define you. We do not have to be victims. It does not mean we're not worthy or have low self-esteem. I couldn't manage the emotions of loving someone who was the aggressor and trying to work through it with them. These moments are transformative opportunities we can learn and move forward from. It's there to reflect on where we were vulnerable and what we can do differently next time. Steve Harvey says that there is a lesson and a blessing in every bad situation. I learned so much about who I was with Tommy and how I needed to grow. Because of that, I'm forever grateful and have made peace with the relationship. And it was from that marriage that I was blessed with my two beautiful children.

***

As a woman bringing life into this world, you become consumed with different sensations. As my daughter grew inside of me, I knew I'd be a good parent. Parenting doesn't come with a manual, but I was determined to be an overachiever as a mother, whatever that looked like. In the same way I tried to overachieve in school and at work.

Julian Olivia was born on September 8, 1990. At the beginning of my pregnancy, I had severe morning sickness. For that reason, I had to take off work for the initial three months. And then one day, it stopped. From then on, my pregnancy was relatively pleasant. I gained twelve pounds over that period (a lot of it was probably from the stress of her father). The rest I'd chalk up to my cravings – those warm, flaky, buttery and cheesy Red Lobster cheddar bay biscuits!

Julian came a week ahead of her anticipated due date. I was in labor for three days, and it was tough. I didn't want to take drugs, and thought that I was doing it the right way. As if suffering is the best thing to do. I was super excited when she was born. She was so beautiful. She reminded me of a China porcelain doll, with her perfectly polished skin and flushed cheeks. Looking down at this beautiful and innocuous being, as she squirmed in my arms while I lay in the hospital bed, I vowed to do everything right by her.

The memories I have with my baby girl are joyous. She was such a good baby, and as my parents' first grandchild, she was embraced by everyone in the family. People wanted to babysit her all the time. I'd dress her up in Rothchild coats, and I knew a woman who had a baby consignment and made dresses. I was a regular in that store, buying countless dresses for Julian. And I loved taking pictures with her. We'd often take them at the photo studios at Sears and JCPenney. Whenever I'd show up to pick up pictures we'd already taken, I'd sign up to get more of us as we waited for the previous set.

It was fun when Julian was little, but she was there during those dark moments I experienced with her father. To this day, it pains me to think about the conditions she was around in the very beginning. She didn't deserve it, and I'm sure there were times when she was super scared, not understanding what was going on. I wish I were more responsible at that time not to have allowed that. But before she turned two, God sent me the final hint that enough was enough.

One day, around Thanksgiving of 1991, I was at my mom's house, standing over the sink in the kitchen washing dishes. As I rinsed the soapsuds from the plate I was holding, my vision became blurry. Feeling light-headed, I slightly tilted my body over the edge of the sink to hold myself up. I let out a faint sigh as my eyes started to close and the weight of my body collapsed on the floor.

I fainted.

When I came to from the sound of my mom's voice, that's when I knew it.

I was pregnant again.

But this was bittersweet.

At that moment, there was only one option. I decided to leave my husband.

CHAPTER 5

Rebirth

M y second daughter saved my life.

Getting pregnant again was not in the cards. During this relationship phase, Tommy, Julian, and I jumped around from one apartment to another because of our many blow-ups. We even briefly stayed with my mom for some time. It was pretty cramped in her two-bedroom apartment. With all of this happening, Tommy and I were barely intimate. Yet there I was, with child once more. It was like an immaculate conception, as though God was protecting and watching out for me.

I'm not bringing another child into this relationship. I am not bringing another child into this chaos.

Realizing another life was growing inside of me, I looked into Julian's eyes. As my firstborn, she meant everything to me. But the stress of dealing with her father was taking a toll. This relationship was impacting other parts of my life, socially and professionally. I thought about my baby shower when I was pregnant with Julian. I'd invited dozens of guests, but hardly anyone came. Because of my relationship, I disconnected myself from many people.

Not only that, but it almost cost me my job. It wasn't unusual for Tommy and me to get into an argument in the mornings as I drove us both to work. From there, it became a domino effect. I'd run late after dropping him off and still had to take Julian to daycare. When I finally arrived at my office, I'd take a moment in the car. Looking into the rear-view mirror, I checked myself over, adjusting my makeup and clothes not to appear disheveled. I had to hide any signs of trouble at home. Then, taking a breath, I'd step out of the car and go inside. On the day I nearly got fired, a bad helicopter accident took out all the power in the city. Even though Tommy and I fought before I came in, I used the helicopter crash as the reason I was late. Again, God was watching out for me because they chose not to let me go.

Between looking at Julian and holding my stomach, I flashed back to the times when Tommy and I were engaged in a screaming match. Julian would observe from a distance, with tears forming. As the bass in our voices grew, so did her screams. I know she was scared and unable to comprehend what was taking place. I once ran out of the apartment to escape Tommy, with Julian at my heels. She toddled outside until the next-door neighbor took her in.

Without Julian, I could have fallen into a deep, dark place. But somehow, she kept my candle burning. Even to this day, that girl looks out for me. I don't know how much longer I would have been in that relationship had I not gotten pregnant with her sister. People must arrive at things on their own, whether overcoming drugs, the wrong relationship, whatever it is. Until that point, I still wouldn't leave or go back, and he and I would find every reason to argue.

SECOND ACT

My unborn daughter became my motivation. I decided the chaos had to stop. I could not do it, not for another minute.

So, I left.

Being discreet and methodical with my exit, I took the day off from work and stayed home to pack everything up. When you've reached the point where you know you're going to leave, pick a day that's right for you. You don't have to make an announcement to the other person or anyone really (unless you want a friend or family member to help you). By the time Tommy got home, Julian and I were gone. We went to my mom's because I knew he would never step foot there. Even though she was a Witness, Mom still didn't play when it came to me, and now, her granddaughter. If I had to get a restraining order, I wouldn't have hesitated to do it (luckily, I didn't need to). Once I decided to leave, I made sure I was willing to do it and never look back. The stuff we used to argue about, all of that furniture and material possessions, didn't even matter. I left it all in that apartment and headed back to my old room at Mom's and slept on the floor.

In some ways, people tend to vilify women who stay in abusive relationships. But just like any other relationship, everyone has their own reasons for sticking with it, something that they're connected to and are trying to hold on for. It's not always about desperation or having low self-esteem or insecurities. It could just be, hey, I love this person, but I don't have the tools to figure this situation out, and I'm just trying to do the best I can. Because who really prepares you for any of this? I held on to my marriage because I didn't want to fail and become the stereotypical single mom. My parents raised me differently, and even though I spent time in public housing, I didn't want to be just another baby momma. In my mind, I felt better than that. But at the same time, it was part of why I stayed. In reality, though, I was failing myself and my child. By letting a fear of failure guide my decision to stay, it was damaging so many other aspects of myself. However, failure, I've learned, is okay. It does not define you.

For anyone who's been battered or in an abusive relationship, hold your head up high. And tell someone. Share your story. Shoot, tell me! There's nothing to be ashamed about. I know it feels like you're all alone in a dark place, but you don't have to be. It's a moment in time. Forgive yourself. Learn from the experience. Once you leave that situation, you will grow. I truly believe that. Whatever you lost will come back one-hundred-fold.

***

Ashton Krista entered the world on July 12, 1992. She was due around September, but my baby made her grand entrance two months early. A testament to her strong-minded personality.

During my second pregnancy, I gained 35 pounds (with two back-to-back pregnancies, you'd expect to gain more weight). Thankfully, I didn't get the same sickness early on like I did with Julian, which I enjoyed. Throughout that time, Julian was a joy. She couldn't contain her excitement to become a big sister and would always talk about the baby.

"Let's read to the baby!" she'd often say, her eyes lighting up.

I could tell she had a sense of protection for the baby and me, no doubt encouraged by her early environment.

Oddly enough, when my mucus plug broke with Ashton, I was with Tommy. On that day, I was at my mom's, and he met me there to help me set up some furniture. Looking back, I wonder if I was agitated or if Tommy's presence stirred up something within me that caused my water to break. Nonetheless, since he was there, he took me to the hospital. We drove to Alta Bates in Berkeley, where I was born, and now both of my children – Julian, after three days of labor and Ashton, twelve hours.

Motherhood isn't something that anyone can prepare you for. I had two different pregnancies, and two individual child-rearing experiences. What worked for Julian didn't for Ashton, and vice versa. In their own unique way, each girl brought separate things to my life, but they were both vital to keep me complete. To me, my children were angelic; I think God just knew I could not, at that time, mentally sustain anything more traumatic going on in my life.

As a parent, I intended for the girls to be their authentic selves. I quickly learned I had to engage each child differently. Their personalities required it. Julian was older and easy because I didn't have to be too hands-on with her. She was the child who potty trained herself. She was much more compassionate and loving, with a cool disposition and a smile always plastered on her face. On the other hand, Ashton rarely parted her lips to show any teeth. She wasn't the sweetest child you'd meet. She didn't talk a lot or walk much until she was three. A bit headstrong, Ashton didn't potty train like her sister and proudly wore her pull-ups until the age of seven. She just didn't care! With her strong personality, Ashton has always been naturally bright without much pushing or prodding.

After leaving Tommy, the girls and I stayed with my mom, where I didn't have to pay any rent and could save money. To make room for her new roommates, Mom moved us from her two-bedroom apartment, the one I grew up in, and into a three-bedroom in the same development. I took the largest room with the girls. At the time, I worked near the San Francisco airport. From Richmond, where my mom lived, along with commuter traffic, it could take more than an hour for me to get to and from work. So mom would take the girls to daycare. If I got stuck and couldn't come back to pick them up on time, she would do it. And even though we didn't live with my dad, he was always around, too. My kids were not in any way, shape, or form deprived of love from their grandparents. All that love that I wasn't sure my mom could give to me, she completely poured into her grandchildren.

**

As a divorcee and newly single woman, I mimicked my mom and didn't date much. I didn't want a bunch of random men around my kids until they got a little older. I was working in the marketing department for a major cellular company at the time, and there was no shortage of amazing men to meet.

Initially, I dated older, married men. Two that I recall. They were relatively wealthy, successful businessmen. I'm not sure if I did it consciously or subconsciously, but looking back, it was my way of protecting myself. My relationship with Tommy took much more out of me than I realized. And my kids were my sole focus. I don't believe that I was in any position to give myself to somebody then. I kept my dating life very casual. Those men would give me money to find babysitters if mom was unable to watch the girls, and we'd go away and do our thing. From my perspective, I was very much like, *'Hey, you got a situation. Our lives don't have to integrate because you got your situation over there, and I'm taking care of my kids over here.'* I was protecting my kids and my heart by all means necessary.

And then I met Winston.

We first connected at a Tony! Toni! Toné! concert when Oakland had their summer outdoor concert series. They were catered to professionals and held on Thursdays after work. At the time, Winston's friend was mysteriously dating my girlfriend. Since they had a mutual connection and already knew each other, my girlfriend and Winston struck up a conversation while we were all hanging out. She introduced him to me, which gave him an opening to slip me his business card.

I took a peek at his card.

Ooo, he's a lawyah.

From a presentation perspective, Winston was suave. He stood at about 6 feet and 385 pounds. Tracing him up and down with my eyes, I noticed Winston was well-dressed and well-manicured. He had the whole metrosexual thing going on. Although he was heavy, he had custom-made suits. Beyond his stature, he had a bit of charisma and confidence, which I later learned was a cover-up for his long list of insecurities. Still, he was personable and intelligent. He had a great sense of humor and knew something about everything. He could talk Biggie one minute and Beethoven and Bach the next. We vibed on so many levels. We probably should've just stayed friends, but, of course, we chose to become intimate.

Being a lawyer and seven or eight years older than me, Winston was the type of person who could be a resource for you. I often asked him for things I needed and sought his advice about life situations. Things like, *what should I do with this opportunity? How do I negotiate a job? How should I strategize about this?* Winston was generous by nature, so I lacked for nothing. But that didn't stop some people from thinking I was taking advantage of him. One reason was that he helped me financially. As a single parent trying to give my children the best, I was open to getting support from the man I was dating. To this day, I am so appreciative of that.

However, underneath, Winston was emotionally unavailable. When I first met him, he was a part of a crew of white-collar guys that were up and coming in the Bay Area – the type who were successful and heavily sought after. None of them were married. Oddly enough, many of them had the mantra that they wouldn't commit or seriously date someone with kids. I was soiled to that crew, and in some ways, it strained mine and Winston's relationship. He was very mindful of what other people thought and said about him. A lot of times, he downplayed our relationship and stepped outside of it, with people that fit into that mold – all flash, no substance.

Winston hadn't seen a good relationship between his parents growing up. Because of that, it was hard for him to give himself to someone. Based on his upbringing, I believe he saw things his parents did behind each other's backs, which never got addressed. As a coping mechanism, Winston was fiercely protective of his image. External validation was super important, and he would not let his emotions get him caught up in a situation that would embarrass him. In addition to that, I also don't think he valued being in a relationship. He always used to tell me how he was a made man, and he could pay for almost everything a woman could do for him. It was like he was dressed in a suit of steel armor, never letting himself get connected to anyone for fear of being hurt.

When I think back, I stayed in that relationship to prove to myself, that even as a single mother, I deserved that type of person and lifestyle. It was all about what looked good and what others perceived as success. You know, all of that external B.S. that really doesn't matter. But to me, it did. I did give some validity to the fact that I was divorced and had two children. I always tried to be and do better to make sure my babies had all the right things. My relationship with Winston reflected my headspace when trying to fit into a social circle or have these people accept me. Sometimes, we go through that, especially in the Black community, with social groups and exclusive organizations. We're always trying to navigate those corners of society and fit in. I stayed in that environment, in some ways to my detriment, but in other ways, to my benefit.

***

I was determined to become a homeowner by 30. And I did, but not how I expected.

I became a first-time homeowner *and* a real estate investor.

In 1998, I was on a Blue World Travel cruise when I met a guy named Theo Williams. Blue World was a Black-owned travel agency in the Bay Area. They were known for starting the "Black" cruise Festival at the Sea, and would sail to different islands in the Caribbean. Theo was in real estate and the one who helped me buy my first condo. It was located on 98th Avenue in East Oakland, on a major thoroughfare, and in a charming condominium community. It was gated, with a grassy area for the kids. I thought of it as a bit of paradise in east Oakland's urban jungle.

But after I bought it, I had second thoughts.

"I can't move my kids in there," I told him.

The condo felt too small for me and the girls with only two bedrooms. When I thought about it, the size of it reminded me of living in an apartment, which I'd done since I was young. I wanted Julian and Ashton to have a bigger space. So I decided to rent the condo and continue my hunt for the right home.

Theo told me he knew of a home he could get me into. Mind you, this was in 1990 when houses cost something like $190,000. With Theo guiding me through the process, he helped me get a loan. By having the condo, I had another stream of income to use for the down payment of the home I ultimately chose. If it weren't for Theo's assistance, I wouldn't have had anyone to help me with the process. My mom didn't know anyone, especially since she never brought a house. Oddly enough, my grandparents owned land, but we never had conversations about how to get into real estate or build wealth at the dinner table. Being the overachieving parent I was, I wanted something different for my children.

I ended up finding my house the following year in a beautiful neighborhood called Maxwell Park, which wasn't too far removed from the center of Oakland. It was a very family-orientated area, with charming Spanish and Mediterranean-style homes. Our neighbors included professors and professionals from Mill College and UC Berkeley. Perched on a hill, the house I chose was on a stunning tree-lined street. There were three bedrooms and two bathrooms. This way, everyone had their own room. There was also a decent-sized backyard area, and plenty of room for the girls to play.

To get this house, though, I had to be creative and have a vision. Unfortunately, the man who lived there at the time of the sale was a hoarder. On the outside, the house was a horrid green color, with overgrown bushes and a cracked retaining wall falling apart. Still, I wouldn't be deterred.

You know what? I'm about to do this.

For support, I called my best girlfriend, Naimah, and explained the offer and what I'd be taking on.

"Don't worry about what it looks like on the outside," she told me. "It's what we're going to turn it into."

I got grown real quick with that house. Because of the hoarding and poor cosmetic conditions, I used that as a negotiation tool. First, I had to clear everything out of the house. Then I repainted it and got the kitchen completely redone. I had gorgeous hardwood floors that were covered and needed to be buffed and stained and I cut down all the shrubs outside. I also got the retaining wall redone. Because of the multiple construction projects I wanted to get done, I learned a lot with that house. There was one time I almost had to sue one of the contractors! Of course, the guys thought they could rip me off because all they saw was a single woman.

As a parent, I patted myself on the back for that one. I could raise my kids in a house in a safe community and not in an apartment in a tense neighborhood like where I was raised. I was immensely proud to reach my goal of becoming a homeowner. Reaching this milestone meant a whole new world of financial ability. A part of it was about my vanity, too. To those who looked down on me as if, as a single mother, I wouldn't be able to make this happen, let alone live in a lofty area, I thought, *look at me now!*

More importantly, buying a home gave me security. I gifted my children with an experience that many young ladies from a single parent household didn't have. For Julian and Ashton, because their mom owned property, I think it added to their confidence. As if to say, *we're not victims because a single parent raises us. We are strong. We are smart. We are independent. We are homeowners.* Representation is super important, and it shows others what we could do. So many people think that as single parents, they're destined not to have things in life. I was the first in my circle of friends to buy a home. A trailblazer in that sense, it set the tone for what excellence looked like amongst our group. Everyone ended up buying homes. It wouldn't be until years later that my friends expressed how they looked at me as an example and inspiration for their own journey. Being able to do that for my friends, who were also single parents, was a feeling like none other.

SECOND ACT

Turning 30 also meant more travel. With those adventures with Mom, like going to Hawaii and the road trips with my grandparents – from Texas to Detroit or California to Arizona – top of mind, I was ready for more exploration. In my late 20s, I started going on Black cruises like Blue World Travel. It was cool, but the satisfaction of those faded quickly. I wanted more. In 2000, I became fast friends with a woman named Lauren. The weekend of my 30th, we went to the Super Bowl in Miami, and let me tell you, we did it up! She and I crashed several celebrity parties around the city. Having fun is always the goal when you're young, and feeling bold and fierce. Not only that, but I was free from my children for the weekend, and going to LIVE!

Besides working as a model, Lauren also had a job for a cruise line that toured Europe and the Mediterranean. One day, she called and invited me to join her, but I initially scoffed at the idea.

"I do not want to go on another cruise," I told her, especially because I had just done a cruise through the Caribbean islands.

"No, Cheri," she said. "We can get off the ship for like three days at each stop."

Now, she was speaking my language.

I ended up traveling with her for three years in a row. We went to Europe and visited London, Rome, and Italy. I'm fascinated with European architecture, and seeing it with my own eyes was simply breathtaking. All those things we hear about, like the ancient ruins in Greece or the art at the Vatican Museums – goodness, gracious—having the privilege to go to these places still blows my mind.

But Lauren and I didn't stop at exploring Europe. We also took a trip across the Mediterranean and went to Tangier, St. Tropez, Canne, and Morocco. Nothing stole my heart more than when she and I touched down in Morocco. That was my first time setting foot on African soil. Going to the mosque, being in areas where they sold all their wares, and enjoying traditional Moroccan food, I truly felt alive. Being on the African continent, felt comfortable. It felt like home. From then on, I vowed to go to the motherland any chance I could. In the years since, I've traveled to other countries, including South Africa, Ghana, and Egypt, and I've always felt welcomed in every place.

There's not one country I've gone to where I've been disappointed. In my eyes, America is not the end-all, be-all. The things that we have issues with in our country is not necessarily everybody's problem. As Black people in this country of African descent, I've found we are so disconnected from culture. When you leave the confines of this place, you'll notice the cultural elements we don't have. That's not to say everything is perfect because, unfortunately, racism and colorism exist in many places. Still, it never sullied my love for adventure. I always find something quaint and unique about every single city that I've visited. Traveling expands your mind. When you try different things, your perspective changes. It adds many layers to who you are, and so much texture to your life. It's why, to this day, I try not to go back to one place more than twice, because there are so many places in the world to see. There's always something to learn, always an experience to have.

CHAPTER 6

To Those I've Tried to Please...

Everyone's parenting experience is unique, but it's also interesting to see how the dynamic between parent and child evolves with each generation. In Daddy Matthew and Mama Opal's era, they believed that children are to be seen and not heard. Questioning authority was blasphemous. Everyone had clearly defined roles.

My mother was raised during the 60s. Her time was split between Chinle, Arizona, during the school months and Tyler, Texas, in the summer, where the stench of slavery was still present. Black people were extremely cautious around white people (Even when I went during the summer as a child, decades later, there were still 'Black only' outhouses). In comparison to my time as a 70s baby growing up in California, there was some hangover from that Dr. Spock way of raising children, but the reins started to loosen up. There was much more leniency and a burgeoning recognition that everyone has a voice, including children.

Mom was not a fan of the philosophy that children should be seen and not heard, yet she was still a disciplinarian. I couldn't run-a-muck, but I had a voice that she entertained. Still, the one thing that impacted her style of child-rearing was religion. The different phases of her life – being in academia, being a Black Panther, and finally, converting to a Witness – came together like a pot of gumbo leaving its mark. She instilled more confidence and Pan-Africanism in me, in contrast to her parents. But after converting, she tried to control and inhibit me in some ways. That's when I'd often hear 'do as I say.'

With my children, I felt a healthy fear was still necessary. I was still a disciplinarian; they had rules to abide by. I was a typical single mom – a school one, to be exact. I was always at the girls' school. If I told them to be outside at 10 o'clock for a party, they had better be outside on time, or else I'd be that mom who would come in and embarrass you. Yet I was also the parent who was there for everything. I was the one whom their friends wanted to hang out with or drop off somewhere. The intensity Ashton and Julian got from me loving and being there for them was the same as I had. In my mind, I was trying to do for them what my parents did for me.

With my dad, I had the autonomy to explore. He was my safe space where I could turn without judgment. Like my relationship with him, I wanted the girls to always feel like they could come to me and have a conversation. Unlike my mom, I didn't want to bring the girls up in a strict religious environment, so I let them be freer. I allowed them to test boundaries to a point. I maintained a boundary. When they were younger, I wasn't going to be their best friend. As a mother, I wanted to make sure the girls did the right thing and made good choices. My parenting style was inspired by what I learned from my religious upbringing around character and morals. Mom raised me to be confident and empowered, and I did the same for Julian and Ashton. I also wanted them to travel and see the world. One of my favorite memories is taking them on an exciting adventure through the lush jungles of Costa Rica. And just like my mom traveled with me when I was young, she took the girls to Mexico to play on beaches with glistening white sands and crystal clear waters.

Still, I wasn't perfect. No parent is. I don't think I became fully comfortable with motherhood until the girls were out of the baby phase. Sure, I wanted to be the ideal mom. But once they started gaining some sense of independence and communicating their needs, like, "Hey, mom, I need to use the bathroom," I let out a sigh of relief.

Cool, I can deal with this.

People have their own opinions about which stage of child-rearing is hardest. What stands out most personally is learning how to navigate two distinct, evolving personalities. Julian, in her younger days, dealt with some awkwardness. She was super tall like I was. Sometimes I could sense Julian was a bit ashamed of her shoe size because she would try to fit in smaller shoes. Like many pre-teens, she also had to grow into her teeth. Her hair was beautiful and thick, but it could become a bit disheveled if I was not on top of it. But I also believe that growing up in an abusive household during those crucial formative years influenced her. She was more easily frightened in comparison to her sister. She took fewer risks and stayed closer to me. I handled her with kid gloves because she was my first, that porcelain doll I didn't want to break. Ashton, on the other hand, was fearless. She didn't care what people had to say. To this day, people love that Ashton's going to say what she means. She's not into pretenses. Overall, they were both great children.

However, that didn't mean they didn't pass up the chance to push limits. There was one time I told Julian to stay inside while I was gone. At this point, we were living in our home in Maxwell Park. While I was away, Julian went outside with one of the neighbors' kids to ride bikes. Since we lived on a hill, it was tempting to ride bikes down it. I'm not sure if she'd ever done it before, but against my directions, Julian decided to take the risk. On her way down, she hit something and flew over the handlebars. She ended up breaking the front of her mouth. Fortunately, she had braces at the time but she broke bones where the teeth were attached. There was skin loose from her face, too. I was a bit surprised when I saw her state when I got home. But I didn't take her to the doctor immediately. To me, this was a teaching moment because she ignored my instruction. I may not have gone about it in the best way, though, because, oh my goodness, was she in pain! Finally, Ashton spoke up.

"Mama, that's too much," she exclaimed. "You've gone too far. You need to take her to the doctor." (I did not long after.)

In relationships between parents and their children, they're not always going to like each other. But you have to accept the whole person. The stuff you can't stand about the other individual is also what you love about them. I think my kids had to swallow many pills because I was intense and had very high expectations of them. And that includes academics. Just as my mom expected of me, I wanted my daughters to do well in school. But Julian had learning challenges that showed up early on. As a kindergartner, she had difficulty grasping concepts. Noticing this, I'd try to guide her through her homework to help her understand things. But she wouldn't get it. As much as I tried to hide it, my frustration became apparent and caused her to cry. Her face would be soaked with tears as I pleaded with her to tell me how I could make everything better. I know she wanted to please me, but I didn't have the temperament to teach things I thought were so easy to grasp. As a young mother, I didn't have the patience she needed from me, and I had difficulty figuring out how to support her. As she got older, I'd get reports back from her teacher that she was acting out as the class clown. I couldn't believe what I was hearing. She was easily distracted, and it wouldn't take long for her to check out. To cover up the fact that she was missing concepts, being a distraction was her way of being cool to her classmates.

Finally, I had Julian tested. We learned she had a processing deficiency, which meant she could only absorb information in small chunks. Once I became aware of her needs, I invested in resources that gave her the foundation to do well in school. I found a tutor and education specialist who worked with children that had similar learning styles to hers. In all honesty, that tutor was not cheap, but I wanted the best. Julian simply required structure and people to teach her the way she needed to be taught. With her tutor's help, Julian began successfully navigating through school. Alongside the other facets of schooling, it became more enjoyable for her. Understanding her learning style boosted her confidence tremendously.

Watching Julian's growth as a student is one of the things I love most about her. She completely embraced her journey. She once told me, "Mom, I understand how I learn. It's different for everyone." She taught me such an important lesson during that time. I wasn't skilled to work with her through her learning challenges without making her feel awful, which was never my intent. Because of that, I didn't hesitate to invest in tutors and programs for her and Ashton when needed. So often, Black children who learn differently get lost in the shuffle and labeled as a problem. That 'one size fits all' way of educating people is not optimal. Kudos to those who can adapt in those environments, but there is more than one way to thrive. The information must be broken down in a way that best suits the child or individual, whether it's auditory, visual, kinesthetic, whatever it may be.

***

The girls and I had our little tribe, but I was blessed with a lot of help. I'd tell myself, *I must be doing something right*, because the community I attracted into my life was nothing but God. So many different sections of people really supported me, from my parents, friends who were also single mothers, and even the Witnesses, whom I reconnected with for a period before I decided to disassociate for the final time. It's because of our village that my daughters were nurtured into star athletes.

Just as I had gone to kindergarten with the Black Panthers, my kids went to a Pan African School in Mosswood Park in Oakland. There was a gentleman there by the name of Brother Harambee. One day, as the children were playing outside, he noticed something about Ashton.

SECOND ACT

"Sista!" he called out to me when I came to pick up the girls. "That little one – those boys tapped her, pulled her hair and tried to run away – she runs them down."

"She's the special one," he added, motioning his head toward Ashton.

Brother Harambee knew of a track team called the 3M track club. The 3M club practiced at Oakland Tech, about a mile from the girls' school. After noticing Ashton's gift, he and his wife, Sister Bathsheba, started walking the kids to practice every day. My baby was phenomenal from the minute Ashton stepped on the track at five years old! Julian didn't start running at first. Being tall and a little gangly, she wasn't interested in it. She was also a girly girl, which further cemented why running wasn't really her thing. Being more of a tomboy, Ashton had no problem with getting sweaty and playing around in the dirt. When Ashton went to practice, Julian sat off to the side, waiting for her to finish. I ended up changing my hours at work so I could pick them up. Before that, Mom would retrieve the girls for me. When I'd get to the track, Julian would join me and sit in the car as we waited for Ashton. Then one day, one of the coaches called Julian out as "wasted talent." Since she was tall, he started working with her, and she eventually ran hurdles.

At first, having two children involved with track was fun. The team, however, was intense. They won a lot, and so there were a lot of expectations. It was like the parents were getting coached, too. You hear about soccer moms? Well, let me tell you, they don't have anything on track parents. It's a commitment, a whole culture,

87

and we were in it. Track season started in April and went through the summer if the team made it to the post-season competition, which my kids always did. The girls also had fall training to build up their base, making track a year long commitment. You were required to be at the track all the time as the children practiced for these small-minute races. We were also on the road a lot, traveling all over the country. There was a meet at least every other weekend and every week during the championship season. Local meet-up days started early, at 6 or 7 in the morning, depending on how far we had to drive. We'd have to pack lunches, snacks, water, sunscreen, hats, foam rollers, extra spikes, and other materials. At the venue, there were two tents, one for the athletes and one for the parents.

Despite the high expectations, I got caught up in the excitement a bit; however, as the parent, I always tried to ensure there was balance. My aim was to make sure they were still doing fun things that they enjoyed, like basketball, ballet, and going to plays. Still, track was king, and training didn't allow for much leeway. I'd like to think I balanced those relationships pretty well. But all that changed when we got to the next level.

We ended up leaving 3M, and the girls started working with a new coach. Curtis Taylor, who trained athletes out of East Oakland's Youth Development Center, is, hands down, one of the best track coaches I know. He took Ashton and Julian on when they transitioned into middle school and stayed with them through high school. He was the one who took them from good to extraordinary. They started performing with international teams worldwide and broke records, receiving numerous accolades. Over her high school career, Ashton won four golds and three silver medals running the 100 and 200 meters. During her freshman year, she set a world outdoor best for 14-year olds in the 100 meters. As a senior, she won the California State 100 and 200 double with national-leading times of 11.17 and 22.90. And in 2010, she was selected as the Gatorade National Track and Field Athlete of the Year. Can you tell that I'm a proud mom?

During that time, outside expectations became overwhelming. I remember being interviewed for the Oakland Tribune, and the reporter asked me how I balanced it all.

"Well, Ashton's a superstar to you guys," I said, "but she still has to take out the garbage at home."

I couldn't control what happened outside, but I always tried to maintain a sense of normalcy at home. The sport takes you over, but the girls were required to do well in school. I did not play with that. I also strongly felt that they needed to remain humble and decent humans. Just because Ashton was a superstar, I wouldn't allow her to become arrogant or belittle people.

As a single mother juggling the careers of rising track stars, my strategy was to have flexibility and create community. Having one is what helped me not become inundated. For work, I'd been in sales for years, and I did so because of the kids' schedule. I remember telling a job I was interviewing for that if I couldn't take my children to track and pick them up, then that company wasn't for me. They extended me an offer and accommodated my schedule. My career was important, but the girls came first.

Parenting is challenging, whether you are doing it alone or within a marriage. However, being a single parent is not victimhood. It does not negate who you are as a person. Society likes to assign negative stereotypes to single mothers or fathers. All it means is that you and the child's other parent do not live in the same household. Honestly, it's not a role you will enjoy all the time. You won't like your kids. You'll think you're doing things wrong, but every parent goes through that. But when those moments happen, because they will, take time for yourself. You're no good to your children if you can't be good to yourself.

My sister circle was one of the first places that reminded me of the importance of putting myself high on my priority list. I have the world's best girlfriends – Robin, whom I met in high school, and Naimah and Tantani from work. They each bring something different to me. Robin is the person I turn to for her wisdom, discernment, and measured approach to advice. Naimah provides the right words at the right time with love and practicality. Talking to her is like getting an affectionate hug. Tantani's optimism and 'it can be done / we can do it' attitude has always been refreshing for me. I get everything I need from the three of them to keep myself mentally, emotionally, and spiritually fed with love and accountability. And we always make room for girl time, whether we're getting massages, facials, or taking a trip. Above all else, we really support each other. Whenever one of us goes through a difficult time, the rest of us come together to strategize how to take care of that person. Having those women around me has been life-saving in many ways.

One time, during a party to celebrate Julian's signing with the University of Michigan, I was asked about the difficulty of raising high-performing children as a single parent. I told them, "One beautiful thing about it is that I can make all the decisions and not have to check with somebody else. If I'm going to take the blame, I want to be driving the train." The level of success my kids have wouldn't have manifested if I had stayed with their father. The few times he'd show up to a meet, he'd try to pick out something wrong, like the positioning of Ashton's arms. Meanwhile, she had broken several records. *Look at him trying to tell me something.* I'd wave off his critiques and instruct him to just be a spectator. I truly appreciate that I could make decisions about the girls without any input. I was able to raise them in the way I wanted to. Maybe that's selfish, but in my case, it brought peace. So if the other parent chooses not to participate or rise up to their responsibility, then it just may be a blessing.

***

Winston and I had so many years of on and off turbulence. He and I first broke up on my 30th birthday because he didn't plan anything special for me. His infidelity was also a point of contention between us. I'd heard stories floating around, and people told me directly. There was a time when he was dating a good friend of one of my girlfriends. She, of course, told me what was going on. Knowing he was stepping out, I'd look through his stuff at his house to find something—anything. Any trust that we had was gone.

Now, here's an example of how two people can be living in two *separate* realities of a relationship:

When Winston and I first got together, he thought I cheated on him. From my perspective, I don't recall us agreeing to be exclusive. I thought we were friends, at the time, since I was dating a professional basketball player. Winston, however, saw it another way and felt that was the ultimate betrayal. This is why, I'd later learn, that being aligned and on the same page is so important. Having clarity is critical to alleviating any misunderstandings. Winston and I remember these events differently. What he felt could've been real for him or an excuse to not be faithful in our relationship. Either way, it wasn't my intent to make him feel that I was intentionally dating someone else while we were together. Neither of us had great relationship and communication tools back then because who really teaches us how to develop them?

But any time Winston's infidelity came up, he would always double back and bring that situation up. As a lawyer, he was always able to argue his point. During an argument, he'd use a term he picked up from a time he visited Thailand: "same, same." It was his way of saying we were the same, so how could I ask him to be faithful if I wasn't? There wasn't any value in having a conversation to address his cheating. He had little to no compassion or accountability for how I felt and never admitted any wrongdoing. I could feel his lack of emotional support in various ways.

So why stick around?

More than anything, it had to do with what I thought about myself and what I believed status looked like. Some of it was about the threat of what other people thought—that we needed to be part of a particular social class or group because of our basic tribal instinct. In my mind, the perception was that I was dating a lawyer. I was good. In reality, it looked bad between us. I told myself that I could try and change him – that, over time, I could *make* him love me the way I wanted him to. It wasn't a good relationship; no matter how much I denied it, many people knew it. The fear of being single was so intense that it transcended my need for healthy, respectable love. Instead, I settled for opening myself up to another troubled relationship. It was like a competition to me. I wanted to *win*. I didn't want the women he was cheating with to get one over on me. My mindset in those days was very reminiscent of the book, *Women Who Love Too Much* by Robin Norwood. Winston was the textbook example of a man, damaged from childhood, trying to protect themselves by avoiding any pain.

Dealing with men back then, I'd see elements in the relationship that would make me think of my dad. But with Winston, our interaction was aligned with that of my mom. Attracting emotionally unavailable men, I now believe, is because I was the same way. Initially, I was dating married men because I didn't want to get too attached. I'd brushed aside the impact of my marriage, but the scars were there. It showed up in the messages I'd tell myself - "Hey, *don't get too invested!*" Tommy was my first real love, and it hurt physically and mentally. It was a failure. I used to ask myself, *how did I end up here?* The effect was that I became more guarded, subconsciously protecting myself. I was intent on navigating life in a way that would serve me better.

Because of that, I was all about my kids. And being raised as an only child, I was also super spoiled. At that point in my life, I hadn't felt the unconditional love I sought. My parents and grandparents showered me with it, but I never found it with the men I interacted with. I approached relationships with the perspective of *what's in it for me?* Instinctively, I was in survival mode. Perhaps it was due to having kids early. I had a vision for my life, and being a mother wasn't going to disrupt that. I had plans to climb the corporate ladder, for instance. Still, having two children was a lot. It's why I was probably attracting people who could help me but not emotionally commit. I naturally gravitated toward people who could provide resources and knowledge to me. I did not want to rely on anyone. Yet, those whom I connected with were successful, a byproduct of their tenacity and intellect. And those individuals satisfied multiple needs I didn't know I had.

Over time, as I became more focused on working on myself, I acknowledged my truth – I didn't have the relationship I wanted. It's not like I only saw bad ones growing up. I knew what good partnerships were. However, I had to face the role I was playing. *Maybe I'm the common denominator in all of this?*

***

When it came to the girls, their grandfather was always reliable. My dad was the type who told them that if there were anything they needed or wanted but didn't get, he'd provide it. He was the one who'd be at the meets and standing on the track taking pictures. Reporters would say, "Mr. Newsome, that section is for the newspaper."

"Well, I gotta get my shot," he'd say turning his attention back to being the girls' paparazzi.

By the summer of 2007, my dad was married to a woman who exhibited insecurities when it came to the kids and me. I can't say with all certainty that she was the reason, but there were some instances when he'd behave strangely. One time, he was supposed to join me and the girls for a track meet in Los Angeles but didn't. When Julian and Ashton were selected for their first world youth team in Ostrava, Czech Republic, my dad was going to buy them iPods for the trip. But he disappointed them again by not coming through. This was unusual for my dad. I was shocked and expressed my disappointment to him. After that, we talked, but sparingly. A lot was going on in that season. Julian was getting recruited for college, and the girls were preparing for their meet in Ostrava.

As the year winded down, I was excited about ringing in 2008 in Salvador, Bahia. A friend of mine owned a bed and breakfast there, and I wanted to go to a party. For some reason, though, I could not pull that trip together. At every step of the way, I hit a block. Either I couldn't get the right flight, or I had to figure out what was going on at work. There was always something that came up preventing me from making arrangements. So I changed my plans and stayed home with the girls, which I was fine with since it was Julian's last year before heading to the University of Michigan. It felt right to lay in bed with my babies, watching all of the New Year's Eve specials and talking about the past year, including our successes and goals for the upcoming one. Just minutes before midnight, I texted my dad, telling him how much I loved him and how excited I was for the upcoming year. There would be so much to look forward to. He texted me back not too long after, echoing similar sentiments.

At one or two in the morning, I got a phone call from a number I didn't recognize. In a split second, I thought about not being able to coordinate my trip, and then I looked back at the number. I knew something was wrong. Although I wasn't standing, it was as if my body had collapsed. My breathing trembled. My heart rate sped up.

When I answered the phone, the person on the other end of the line told me they were from the hospital.

"Ms. Syphax," they began, "We're calling to tell you…"

My dad was gone.

Those text messages we exchanged at midnight was the last time we'd ever speak to each other.

***

My dad passed doing what he loved—enjoying life.

I later learned he was preparing to go to a New Year's Eve party. While he was in the bathroom getting ready to go out, he collapsed. He had a pulmonary embolism and no one could resuscitate him. My friends used to call me a witch, but what they didn't get was that I have a strong intuition. It wasn't by happenstance that I was unable to get to Brazil. You're talking about somebody who could make a trip happen in a heartbeat. Back then, I couldn't understand what it was about this one that I couldn't make work. And then I found out why.

Nobody saw this coming. My father's wife, now widowed, was a mess. At the hospital, she couldn't say a word. My brothers were traumatized. When my dad texted me, there was nothing wrong. And then that was it. Until then, I always tried to make sure I didn't show emotion or break down. I was determined to be the strong one, but this broke me all the way down. All I remember is being in a fog for a long time.

As my dad's oldest child, I wanted everything perfect for his homegoing. I was the family's point of contact to ascertain everyone knew what was going on. My phone was constantly ringing and chirping from notifications.

What's the plan?

What are we doing?

I had nothing left to give, and my patience was wearing thin. I nearly lost it when my mom hinted that she wouldn't attend the funeral because it was at a church. (Witnesses do not go to places of worship outside of the Kingdom Hall, but there is flexibility for attending things like weddings and funerals. It's completely up to the individual. Mom would've been making a conscious decision not to go.)

"You will not not come to my dad's funeral," I said sternly. "There's no way on this planet that you won't be there to support the girls and me."

"You take this religion stuff way too far," I added. Then emphasizing that she would not be going to church to worship but instead honor my father, I gave her an ultimatum.

"I ask you to think long and hard about making this decision, because this will be the ultimate deal breaker." Thankfully, she chose to be by our side.

My dad's homegoing was painful but celebratory, a homage to his life. The church was full of family and friends. The girls, my siblings, and my dad's widow sat in the front pews. I remember the pastor, who eulogized my father, mentioning how difficult of a day it was because he had to bury his friend. So many of the people that my dad touched throughout his life – an ode to who he was – came through for me and the family. They helped to coordinate a beautiful repast in his honor. Even though countless people were in view, they were all a blur. I sat in the front row, looking at my dad in his casket. He was so handsome, as he always was, dressed in a stunning dark suit. As he lay there in front of me, sleeping peacefully, I silently spoke to him.

Rest well. You've done good. Thank you for being an amazing dad to me.

My dad was my biggest cheerleader. My refuge. My rider. The part that gives me solace is that he lived his life boldly, out loud, until his final moments. He was the life of the party, his swagger undeniable. He was my other half, the fun, effervescent, and gregarious part of me. In those early days following his passing, it felt like a part of me died with him.

CHAPTER 7

Divine Timing

For many women, turning 40 is a time of reflection, to reassess who they are and what they truly want out of life. Some call it a decade of unlearning and redefining yourself; sometimes, the catalyst is after a major life event like divorce, getting remarried, becoming an empty nester, or having children for the first time. Others declare it as the season when they started having more confidence, embracing their flaws, and giving little to no F's. They start honoring their needs over pleasing other people.

I felt a mental shift when I crossed into my fourth decade, the type where I felt like I was officially grown, grown. At that point, Julian was away at college. Ashton was entering her senior year of high school and choosing which university she wanted to go to. Transitioning into my empty nester phase of life felt liberating. I had lived so close to my children's success and tended to their every need. After all of that, I was ready to have more freedom and check off more milestones. In my mind, 40 was going to be a celebration, and I was going to have all kinds of fun!

However, there was a part of myself that felt like I hadn't quite gotten **there** yet, like I had everything together. I was still somewhat reeling from my father's death two years earlier. And I hadn't quite gotten my rose-colored glasses off about Winston. I kept forcing the relationship, but I was certain that it would help our relationship tremendously once the girls left home. Even though I wasn't 100 percent satisfied with my life at that point, I was optimistic about the future. But that didn't stop God from sending me a sign forcing me to seriously reconsider how I was living life.

I was 42 when Julian was heading into her graduation year at the University of Michigan on a track scholarship, while Ashton went to the University of Miami as the number one sprint recruit for the Miami Hurricanes. Unfortunately, she never got the chance to run for them. Before the season started, she got injured. She had a tear in her rectus abdominis – a psoas muscle injury, which is difficult to come back from. My schedule turned frantic as I stepped in to support her. I was on the phone constantly, and I flew from California to Miami three times to get face time with her doctors to help arrange her physical therapy. It was the first time Ashton was hurt, and there was a bit of anxiety about the unknowns surrounding the situation. Her coaches and I could not agree on a treatment option, as they wanted her to have surgery. But being that Ashton was one of the fastest in the world and never been hurt before, I wasn't in favor of that suggestion.

We decided it would be best for Ashton to come home to California. She would transfer from the University of Miami to the local community college where her high school coach taught and coached the track team. In some ways, she might have thought this was quitting. Ashton loved being in Coral Gables and did not want to leave school and her friends. It was disappointing going through the recruiting process and finally settling on a school, only to never suit up for it. What would people think about going to a Division I school and then transferring to a junior college? Ultimately, my children are not quitters, and she knew this move was for the best. And it was. Her school went on to win the junior college title and Ashton won the 100 meters, 200 meters, and 4x100 relay. She also set a record in the 200m. But when I tell you how the universe works in your favor! Little did I know, having Ashton home with me would turn out to be divine order.

Thinking back on that time, I went into my 40s anticipating my freedom. But some of that had to be put to the side to support my daughter. As someone who gets super focused on whatever is on my plate, especially concerning my kids, it made Winston feel a type of way. He didn't explicitly say it, but the vibe I got from him was, *wait, hold on. I thought it was going to be you and me, but you're still dealing with your kids.* In those days, I thought I was a good partner. I believed I was doing things right. But in reality, I wasn't giving the relationship the time it needed, and I wasn't in tune with what Winston needed from me. It's imperative to be self-aware in relationships, and understand how we are showing up for the other person, and how we are not.

I think as women, oftentimes we don't see ourselves. By taking on the superwoman image, we make sure everyone else is taken care of, but we fall to the bottom of the list and neglect our own needs. I was no different. I'd make sure the girls made it to all their appointments, from chiropractors to tutors. Meanwhile, I wasn't even getting routine checkups. I hadn't gotten a physical in maybe five years. In my mind, I was a pretty healthy person – since the girls ran track, I cooked, and we ate well. To stay active, I'd walk the track while the girls worked out and go to the gym with my friends to do light weight and cardio workouts. I thought that was sufficient. But the reality was that I wasn't caring for myself as much as I should have. It wasn't until Ashton and Julian were off at college that I finally went to get a physical.

Around my birthday, in January 2012, I had my first mammogram. That's when the doctor told me they saw something. Hearing the news, I didn't think much of it. Being somewhat optimistic, I couldn't fathom having breast cancer. The challenge was that I didn't have a baseline since this was my only mammogram. Up until that point, I wasn't someone who did breast checks. I didn't have a history of it in my family, so there wasn't a reason for me to do early breast examinations. I just figured the testing wasn't clear, so the doctor would need to do more and confirm everything was fine. I was asked to come back for a follow-up and did my biopsy around Valentine's Day.

A week later, at 1:30 in the afternoon, I got a phone call. When I answered, the woman introduced herself as Heather. She was a nurse, and her voice was pretty perky and upbeat. I thought she was going to tell me that the lump the doctor found was benign.

"Ms. Spigner," she said. "Your results were positive for ductal carcinoma in situ."

Hearing those words, my body went numb. Heather continued, saying something about the next steps…and surgery…and how I needed to decide on a course of treatment. But I couldn't fully listen to anything she said. I was in a daze. It was surreal, like an out of body experience. As I sat with the phone hanging on my ear, all I could think of was how I'd convinced myself that my mammogram came up abnormal because I had deodorant on. I downplayed that large amount of calcification had been found in my breasts. I thought, *so many people get biopsies, and they are usually negative and mine would be too.* Wrong. The fact was I had breast cancer. My stomach sank, and I started to panic.

Am I going to die?

Do I have to do chemotherapy?

Won't that cause me to be sick and lose my hair?

Would I need a mastectomy?

Without breasts, will I still be attractive?

Will I make it to Julian's graduation?

As tears started running down my cheeks, I cried, "Why me? Why me?" My foundation was disturbed. I felt vulnerable. Alone. Afraid. And helpless. For the first time in a long time, I was unsure where my life would go or if I'd even live. You think about how you're living your life, and, for the most part, you believe you're healthy. Until that point, I never had any issues that told me otherwise. But the first time I dealt with an ailment or disease was cancer. Cancer feels terminal when you first get the diagnosis. It's scary when you think of how so many people die from it. But after the initial shock wears off, you realize it doesn't necessarily have to be.

After my meltdown, I pulled myself together. *Breathe, Cheri. Breathe.* This news wasn't going to overtake my life. Julian was scheduled to graduate in April. My beloved who learned differently and blossomed from a girl to a woman at one of the best academic institutions in the country. There was no way I was going to miss my firstborn getting her degree! I learned that ductal carcinoma in situ (DCIS) is considered the earliest form of breast cancer. Luckily, it isn't stage one cancer, but it means that the cells that line the milk ducts have become cancerous and have not yet spread to the nearby breast tissue. Knowing that I was going to be working with my doctor on a treatment plan, the thought never entered my mind that I wouldn't be at Julian's graduation. She didn't see it that way, though.

"Mom, do you need me to come home?" She asked when I shared the news with her.

"Absolutely not!" I countered without hesitation. "You will graduate. I need you to walk across that stage in April."

There was no way I would let Julian come home and compromise everything she had worked for. She went from having a learning difficulty to one of the best schools in the country and was eligible to graduate in four years. I wasn't going to let her toss that aside, nor was I missing the opportunity to be there to support her as a proud parent. And that's how we were going to roll. I was resolute that no one would fall apart because I had cancer—especially the girls, who still had their lives to live.

Although DCIS isn't considered an emergency, it's still precancerous. You have to choose between treatment options.

Those may include breast-conserving surgery combined with radiation or surgery to remove all of the breast tissue. I had the choice to do aggressive chemo and radiation. But I saw how it could debilitate people since the healthy cells are killed along with the cancerous ones. I wasn't for having any of those treatments or injections. Therefore to absolve myself from all of that, I asked about a radical mastectomy. I'd done the research and found that people who have hereditary breast cancer in their families do that as a preventative measure. I didn't want anything lurking around, which is why I wanted to go that route.

Still, I definitely had some hesitations. I thought about what it would be like not having breasts. As women, we are constantly judged on certain aspects of our bodies. Since Winston and I didn't have the greatest relationship, it felt like this was going to be one more thing for me to be insecure about. Luckily, I had great doctors. After talking through my options, I got excited. *I'm doing a radical mastectomy – just take 'em all!* In my mind, I was going to get two new boobs! I had no reason to have a breeding ground for cancer cells. And since I had breastfed my kids, my boobs were saggy. Heading into the procedure, I thought about it as, *I'm going to have good perky breasts!* One doctor was going to do my mastectomy, and the other, my plastic surgeon, would do my implants. "Whatever we're going to do, I need to do it quickly," I told them. "I need to be in Ann Arbor, Michigan on April 12th." And that was the plan. To show up in Ann Arbor with some good tatas! My doctors knew the assignment, and they executed it. My surgery happened in early March.

Unfortunately, my recovery did not go smoothly, jeopardizing my trip to Ann Arbor. My left breast, which had the DCIS, rejected the implant. My frustration elevated as the complications started. It's like, you go from having one of the worst diagnoses ever to thinking that you are healing, but then your progress is derailed. With a little under a month until Julian's graduation, I didn't know if I was going to make it. I had to get two surgeries to try to salvage the implant, but ultimately, circulation was bad. I had to remove my breast once I developed necrosis, a condition when the skin dies.

By the grace of God, I was on the flight to Michigan in April. The trip was taxing on me as I was still recovering. But that didn't take away from how amazing it was to see my first child graduate. Not only am I a college snob, but I was a total fan of the Fab Five (University of Michigan's 1991 men's basketball team), Charles Woodson and Desmond Howard. They both played football at Michigan during their college years. I was ecstatic, not only when Julian chose to go there but also that she was graduating in four years. She had three ceremonies – the traditional celebration at Michigan stadium, known as "the Big House," a ceremony for the African-American students, and the other in her academic discipline. Julian gained an abundance of confidence at Michigan, and it was such an accomplishment for her to get her degree. My mom, brother, and sister-in-law were there with me. We got to spend time in Detroit, about 45 minutes away from Ann Arbor, to do some sightseeing. My uncle, my mom's brother, lived in Detroit then, and we all met to have dinner together. Despite my physical complications, that trip was worth it a hundred times over.

Back home, I had to deal with the aftereffect of losing my breast. Most women deeply connect to the external symbols that help identify us as women. Because of the issues, I now had the option of getting a prosthesis. The thought of that terrified me. *How would it look? How would I look?* I ended up wearing one for a couple of years until I got reconstructive surgery. During this procedure, the fat is taken from other parts of your body to rebuild the breast. As a gift to myself, I scheduled the surgery on my birthday, January 26, 2015. The doctor who performed the surgery described it to me as taking "plumbing" from my stomach and rerouting it up to my breast. In other words, they took fat from my stomach, and to this day, I have a scar between my pelvic bones, almost as if I had a tummy tuck.

Because of the failed surgery and rebuilding my breast with fat instead of a perky implant, I have uneven breasts. The right one is bouncy and sits high. But the left one? Not so much. Basically, fat is not going to look like saline in a balloon - ha! Even still, the left one is my favorite. It always reminds me that I am a thriver, regardless of anything. The scars, they're here, but they can't stop me. It's why in 2015, I did a bikini competition for Breast Cancer Awareness month. Motivated to inspire other women, I stood up on that stage and put my body on display, flaws and all. I wanted to prove to other women that they were still worthy, regardless of their literal or figurative scars. I had to show that you don't have to let anything deter you from just showing up and being your most incredible, best self. I wanted to let women know — those who were fighting insecurities, suffered loss, abuse, or felt alone — that I saw them. They do not have to suffer in silence. I was a public expression of victory. I had overcome abuse and cancer. My new normal is of a scarred body that reflects its journey, which I am so proud of.

If reconstruction surgery is an option for you, be sure to research who will perform it, because it can be a very complex one. If you have a great surgeon, build a relationship with them. And if you don't have one, get referrals. The procedure was one of the best things that I did. Since my body didn't want the implant from my first surgery, it replaced it naturally. Because of the challenges I had with the necrosis, I have some deformation. But overall, it feels and looks natural. And I am proud that I have these two breasts. They tried to take me out, but I didn't let them. And I've made peace with them.

***

The first time I got a sign to change my life was when Ashton entered this world. The second? Breast cancer. I haven't done any research on this, but there's a book called *Cancer Saved My Life* by Lois Berry. I believe that breast cancer made me look hard at my life and be real with myself. I wasn't completely oblivious to my circumstances and how I felt about them. Yet there was no catalyst to make me stop and recognize that *I needed to sit back and look at my life.* When life is okay, we tend to roll with it. But cancer? Oh no. I had to reevaluate where I was trying to go and what I was trying to do.

At a point in life, we may find toxicity around us, whether it's from a relationship, a friendship, or work. As mature women, we know when things no longer serve us. We know when it's not the right partner or job. At the time of my diagnosis, I wasn't thriving at work. I wasn't inspired by what I did and had no passion. And that can drain you. Add to that how unhealthy my relationship

SECOND ACT

was with Winston. All of that absolutely contributed to stress and other health problems.

I knew I was not where I was supposed to be. I didn't have boundaries or balance. I'd work 12 hours a day, and give my kids all my spare time and attention. I was up early, checking email and taking the girls to school. After that, I'd either go straight home to my office or go to an appointment for work. I'd work until it was time to pick the girls up from school. While I waited for them, I might walk the track or stay in the car, following up on calls and emails. Once track was over, I'd take the girls to their tutor. Once their homework was done, we'd go home, and I'd cook dinner. After eating, it was time for baths, prepping for the next day, and setting out clothes for school and work. Before I closed my eyes, I'd check my email once again. I rarely made time for myself. I knew all of this, but I was still going with it. It's easy to stay in our bubble or the box we've created for ourselves. Nothing radical enough happened before my diagnosis to shake me up and force me to move past comfort and mediocrity. My diagnosis was a pivotal moment. My lifestyle was killing me. Being in the wrong relationship, the job I hated, and not being fulfilled in my life. I wholeheartedly believe that my body was telling me it didn't like what was going on and that I needed to change, and here was my wake-up call to do it. It shook me to the point where I acknowledged I wasn't living this fabulous life that my dad always told me I should be living. It was time to live a life I felt destined for and deserving of. I'm trying to live fabulously every day. And if I die tomorrow, I know I'll have lived a good life.

Although it was a challenging period, that life lesson saved me. It was the setup to shift my mindset around my life and what I wanted out of it. It's what started my journey of exploring my spirituality differently and seeking out a life coach and health practitioner. I was on a quest to find inner peace. Life is about looking at everything as an experience because it's there to teach you something. From that period on, I vowed never to do anything I wasn't passionate about, or anything I didn't want to do. If I'm feeling too stressed, if I'm feeling like something's not meeting my needs, or if anything is not aligned, I release it. I think as Black women, we take on all the concern in the world, and it kills us. And that's really what breast cancer did for me. It taught me something so powerful that when things don't feel good to me, I listen to them. When we're in tune with our bodies, it serves as a barometer that tells us what we need to know. Taking care of your body and making time for yourself is paramount. For our health, preventive care is crucial. If you have insurance, there's no reason not to get your annual checkups, especially as we grow older. We work hard to have good insurance. Use it. Be selfish and make time for yourself in that way.

So many women prove how not only is there life after cancer, but we can also thrive after beating it. No matter how challenging it is at one time or another, it truly comes down to your mindset and the people around you. I was truly blessed to have people that stood up for me during that time. My best friend Naimah took me to get my mammogram (on her birthday) and my follow-up appointment. My girlfriends from Kensington put together a food tree and brought meals weekly. Other girlfriends and family members, like my brother and sister-in-law, came and spent time with me. Even Winston was a trooper through all the iterations of what was happening with me and my body. My job at the time was super supportive, too. I've always wondered if I'm as good of a friend to other people as they are to me. Yet whenever I've been in a situation, people have shown up for me. Building a support system around you for those challenging moments in life will help you get through it.

Regardless of the obstacles, we must live. We do not know when the last day is. Every day I say, if this is my last one, I want no regrets. I try to live to the maximum of my capacity and enjoy it. In life, I say be bold in everything. Even if that means speaking up to say, hey, I'm not feeling good, or sharing something you've overcome. Please don't feel like you can't because we hold things in believing any show of emotions makes us weak. We don't want to be a burden on others, so we act as if we are okay or that we got it. But in actuality, vulnerability is strength. The more we share, it makes you realize other people have gone through stuff, too. You're never alone. Let others know your truth because your testimony can motivate or inspire someone. People don't even know what I look like underneath these clothes, but I've got an assortment of issues. I'm all kinds of deformed around here. But that surgery saved my life. Your literal and figurative scars don't have to define you. Despite those scars, you are still BEAUTIFUL.

CHAPTER 8

Higher Ground

My heart broke when my mom chose not to support me in going to college. In my last year of high school, I'd count down the days until I was officially an undergraduate student, especially when I got accepted into UCLA. I used to imagine strolling the campus yard with my bookbag across my shoulders, textbook and notebook inside bouncing against my back. I'd picture myself in the library late at night with my study group as we shared notes to cram for the next day's midterm exam. I visualized being in the lecture hall of my favorite class, sitting up front and taking notes as I absorbed every concept the professor taught. Not only were those dreams deferred, but they also worked out differently than I envisioned.

Eventually, my mom buckled and offered a compromise – she'd allow me to go to UC Berkeley because the university was close to home. Though they initially denied my application, Berkeley agreed to accept me after a phone call from mom. To this day, I have no idea what she told them. By that point, I was drained from the whole situation. I was so excited about UCLA that although Berkeley is an excellent school, I was disappointed and not inspired to attend. I wanted to get away, and living at home and attending college was not what I had in mind. Ultimately, it turned out that we didn't complete enough of the critical paperwork for Berkeley, so school was deferred indefinitely. The embarrassment would weigh on me for years. I never thought something could derail me from going to school, and having to navigate the aftermath of that was tough. Looking back, I now see that point in my life as a test. Later on, independent of attending UC Berkeley for undergrad, I got a marketing certificate. It was fitting since I was in a marketing role at my job. The program was intense, and it satisfied my continual quest for knowledge and desire to learn.

School came about twelve years later, around 2000. That vision I had of Cheri, the carefree university student, turned into Cheri, the working, single mother of two young children who went to college part-time. I went to Holy Names College, which today is known as Holy Names University, a private Roman Catholic-based school in Oakland. At the time, they had a new program for working professionals who needed non-traditional hours to go to school. I'd go to class a couple of nights a week and sometimes on weekends. On Tuesdays and Thursdays, I'd leave work promptly at 4 p.m. and spend an hour in traffic to make it to campus by 6 p.m. Class would let out by 10 p.m. I was exhausted from the long days, but luckily our home in Oakland was only 10 -15 minutes from school.

For the most part, my relationships with my professors were pleasant. Still, with the responsibilities I juggled outside of the classroom, I had to over communicate regularly with my teachers, though sometimes, I had to get creative and flex my negotiation skills. For example, one of my required classes was statistics, and for some reason, I struggled with the work. At the time, I was an analyst at Cellular One. I was doing promotion results and demonstrating how effective our advertising was. (To put it simply, this was applied statistics.) But no matter what I tried, I could not pull it together for that class. So, I approached my professor with a proposal.

"Hey, I do this every day at work," I explained. "For some reason, I just can't figure out how to pass the test. I use these principles at work. Could I bring in what I'm doing and do a presentation on that?"

And he did.

I remember another class, Inner Disciplinary Studies Across Cultures (ISAC), as one of my favorites. It had four sections that covered the ancient world, the pre-modern world, the modern world, and the contemporary world. We also studied art in Europe, and I couldn't get enough of it. When I started school, Julian and Ashton were about 10 and 8, and there were times when I couldn't find a babysitter for them. Sometimes, after work, I'd make a detour to the girls' school to pick them up on my way to campus. I'd walk into class carrying a satchel with my materials for class and the girls following at my heels. I reminded them to stay quiet as I located seats for all three of us and settled in for the evening. I made sure to be transparent with my professors. However, there was one instance when I was late with an assignment, and my ISAC instructor ripped into me about my delayed homework. I was the type who would try and talk my way into and out of stuff, but in this case, that man would not budge when I asked for extra time to get the work done.

Okay, no problem, I thought.

So, what did I do? I brought the girls with me to class for the rest of the semester.

One day, he finally approached me at the end of the term. "I am so sorry," he said. Sometimes, you got to show people what you can't tell them. I think it's hard for some folks to imagine all that a person has to manage outside of class, which is why my kids were right there in school with me. And I finished that semester with good grades!

Overall, my rapport with my teachers worked well because of my maturity, and I applied what I was learning. Despite being delayed a decade, I achieved what I set out to do. At 34, I finished school and got my bachelor's in 2006.

Since I love learning and being in school, I toyed around with the idea of getting my Master of Business Administration (MBA). I came across St. Mary's College six years after getting my undergraduate degree. A private Catholic college in Moraga, California, it's located in a serene, ritzy area. The type of place where high schools look like college campuses. I was in awe of St. Mary's campus, but they didn't have a non-traditional MBA program. It wasn't until I ended up meeting with one of the professors in the Department of Leadership that I was sold on the idea of enrolling there. Not for an MBA, though. I decided to go for a master's in leadership and organizational behavior. I knew it was the right program for me when I attended orientation. We didn't talk about typical introductory topics. We focused on mediation. Since my breast cancer diagnosis sparked my spiritual journey, the alignment between my personal development and the curriculum was perfect.

Honestly, I didn't care what they taught me. I just enjoyed being in that space. As a single parent of two children, life was hectic. In contrast, I could go to campus and take a workshop on mindfulness. It was just what I needed. It was like the universe brought this program to me precisely on time. It was a case of when the student is ready, the teacher shows up.

To be a good leader and guide others, you have to know who you are – and my master's program forced me to go deep. It required me to look at myself more intimately than I had before. The program made me tap into who I was, identify my core values, and assess how I showed up in the world. We did a lot of value assessments and personality tests. I already knew mine: driver and overachiever. What I hadn't done much work on was my value system. Those assessments showed me that comfort, security, and familiarity were strong needs for me.

That program also stretched me in how I navigate conflict in relationships. In one of my classes, I clashed with another woman. Back then, I was doing a lot of stuff – working full-time, traveling to track meets to be a guide, support system, and consultant for the girls, and running for the Oakland school board. I was barely at school, but I was still performing well. I knew how to pull it all together when I had to, and this woman hated that. Some people don't like that things come easy to others. (However, I will add that that's also a detriment. School shouldn't come easy. You don't take it as seriously when something becomes too easy.) One of the requirements of our class was doing modules online, and she took a moment to call me out one time. My first reaction: *Don't hate!* But I knew there was a better way to resolve things. It was a helpful situation because, as I moved into leadership roles in my career, being someone with tools to resolve conflict was always beneficial. And I attribute that to my master's program. It was money well spent and one of the best decisions I made.

Although the program focused on knowing yourself as a leader, those principles also translated into daily life and interpersonal relationships. It's difficult to articulate to someone what it looks like to love or treat you if you don't know who you are and what you need, like, and require. The second lesson I took away was understanding how I show up. I recognized that being in that academic environment with people different from myself presented instances when my presence rubbed others the wrong way. It's not that I have to shrink myself, but I also don't have to blind people with my light all the time. There's no advantage or value in that. My dad used to tell me, "I don't care if your light shines bright –burn 'em! Make them put on sunglasses." That was useful to tell a young child to build up her confidence, but there comes a point when that outlook no longer works. You can attract many more people when you're self-aware of how you impact them. Essentially, it's okay to meet people where they are.

My master's program helped me see how effective and impactful leaders can be while remaining modest. When you think about people like former President Barack Obama, Mother Teresa, or Mahatama Gandhi, they're super humble individuals, but their words are powerful. Power doesn't necessarily come from those who are the loudest or the strongest. Gandhi definitely didn't come across as this big, strong viral man. And that's how I now govern myself in dealing with friends and family. I can always be the first one to try and reach across the aisle, so to speak, and apologize. I used to have a need to be right and always defend my position. But I learned that wasn't necessary. I don't always have to prove I'm the smartest person in the room. It's fine to allow somebody else's idea or opinion to be highlighted at times. I can listen to others with the goal of understanding versus reacting and proving my point. Sometimes, it's hard for us to let go and concede especially as women. But I've found that utilizing those skills in both my personal and professional world has led me to have stronger bonds.

***

My need to overcommit and overachieve in every area of my life manifested with my decision to run for the Oakland school board. In hindsight, it was also tied to my desire for validation, for someone to say, *hey, she's the bomb!* That was part of it, but I was also driven by my incessant passion for education and my children's experience in the school system. As a homeowner in Oakland, I had significant tax obligations in the city, but the school system was not one I felt my children would thrive in. Ideally, I wanted my children to have my Kensington Elementary School experience. I tried public and charter schools, but ultimately my children went to private schools. I believe public school should be just as good as any other school. An excellent education should be accessible to all, regardless of zip code. While I lived in a good neighborhood, those who did not, had fewer options for a free education. I also thought about Black women, single mothers especially, who may not have the confidence, support, or know-how to navigate the school system. It requires a lot. I considered those who don't have room in their budget to send their kids to private school. Lastly, I reflected on this one-size-fits-all teaching environment and how it does not work. We all learn differently. Though I didn't think that I could revolutionize the way children are taught, I did feel like my voice could be heard if I at least had a seat at the table.

As a candidate in my district, I based my platform on being the only one in a race of four who had a strong business and technology background, despite being a political outsider. My position was that I would be the best candidate to analyze the district's finances, a necessary perspective that was missing from the board for quite some time. Endorsed by organizations like the Black Young Democrats and Black Women Organized for Political Action, I raised over $16,000 in contributions. If I'm not mistaken, that was more money than any other person in the race, including those backed by labor unions.

Jumping into the school board race was scary yet interesting. From that experience, I realized that politics is tricky. It's not entirely fixed, but you'll find there's a candidate already groomed to win. I saw how people weren't necessarily supporting who they thought was the best candidate. People were supporting candidates based on their self-interest. For example, suppose a person worked for union-backed trades, the union might automatically endorse them, regardless of their experience or platform. I wasn't a labor candidate, so I didn't get those endorsements which can be critical to political success. And that's what a lot of politics is about, unfortunately. In no way am I encouraging you not to have faith in our democracy. However, I believe we must be aware of how the game is played. If you want change, you have to get involved, especially on the local level. Unfortunately, some of us tend to forget how local politics are much more impactful to neighborhoods, cities, and counties than the presidential election.

I've come to see that everything I did up to that point in my life was to prepare me for the next thing. I'd never done anything like stepping out on faith and running for school board. Still, I was always active in the political process, including being part of the National Coalition of 100 Black Women and Black Women Organized for Political Action. I also volunteered for EMERGE, an organization that helps women develop into political leaders. I'm certainly a political junkie in that way, and I always want to see women, especially Black women, succeed.

Although I lost the race, that experience gave me two things – I now know the intricacies of politics and can help others. It also prepared me for my next career.

***

I was 24 when I started working at Cellular One. In the mid-90s, McCaw Cellular and AT&T owned half of Cellular One. I got the job through my girlfriend's godmother, who coached me through the interview process. Diane, a Black customer service manager, wanted to see more people that looked like us at the company. On average, folks there were making around $40,000 a year, which was pretty good money when talking about some 20

– 25 years ago. I was coming from Wells Fargo Bank, where my annual income was $24,000.

As Black women in corporate environments, we know all too well about the pressures to navigate white spaces and assimilate. Still, no matter how you move, when people are intimidated and want to pull the rug out from underneath you, they will. I remember a woman in customer service who detested me, and ended up managing me. Alongside the woman who was the head of the department, neither of those ladies liked my shine at all. Customers used to call and specifically ask for me and people around the department would come to me with questions. I think that threatened those women. So much so that my manager tried to falsify documents about my review and say that I had a terrible one so I could get fired. I was completely caught off guard because my previous evaluation was stellar. It was uncomfortable, to say the least. It's like knowing something you can't control, like your confidence and presence, can intimidate people so much that they try to harm you.

Unfortunately, back then, as a 24-year-old with two young kids, I didn't have the self-assurance to think I could get another job. I needed that one. I raised the issue to human resources to initiate an investigation, and I was moved into the marketing department. That change turned into a great experience, but it was also compensation to keep that situation with my former manager hush, hush. But if I knew then what I know now, I would have definitely sued them.

This experience is far from unique; as Black women, we're quickly denounced as threatening without even knowing it. But to feel comfortable in a white, corporate space, I did the usual – varied how I spoke, always wore suits, and pretended to like the same music and TV shows. I understood how to navigate since my mom sent me to Kensington, a predominantly white elementary school. I was one of a few Black students in advanced classes in junior and senior high school. However, what that doesn't allow for you to be your authentic self. When I decided to leave Cellular One about five years later, I went to work for AT&T. Although I loved working there, I still never really felt like my true self. And it's exhausting and emotionally draining.

Being in the telecom industry for a long time, I had plenty of highlights at AT&T. I learned how to sell technology. It pushed me out of my comfort zone because I oversaw corporate accounts and interfaced with CEOs, CFOs, and folks in IT. I used to have accounts for Google and Salesforce. Girl, if I knew then what I know now, I would have invested $100 each into both and be rich right now!

I'm still connected with many of the people I met at AT&T (Cellular One). I built many relationships with mentors and met my two best friends there, Naimah and Tantani, who were there with me every step of the way. It was a great company, and I am proud to have been there. But, as the years carried on, my old values crept up.

By 2014, the writing was on the wall. I hated my job. It had been years that I was unmotivated and uninspired with my work. It was mundane, but I was comfortable. I'd had my accounts forever, so my performance was okay. Initially, I had no idea that my time at

SECOND ACT

AT&T was coming to an end. I got the memo, though, when I was put on a performance plan. I knew I had to turn it around.

Okay, wow, they put me on this plan. I've got to hit a certain target by such and such date, I thought.

Since I had my accounts for so long, I figured I could make some things happen fast. And I did. I hit my target right before Thanksgiving. You'd think meeting the task would take me off plan, but it didn't. AT&T was constantly restructuring, and I got caught up in the bigger plan. They were either trying to manage people out or give folks early retirement packages because they had been downsizing for years. When I didn't get taken off the plan and put on an extended one through the holiday season, that's when I knew they were trying to let me go. Imagine trying to hit a target during this time, when major decision-makers are away, and many companies in Silicon Valley shut down for the last two weeks of the year.

Let me ride this out as long as I can, I decided. I'd already planned a trip to South Africa, which was divine timing because the universe always works things out. The company did try to get me on a conference call to let me go. But I was on vacation, so that plan was a bust. I did that purposely to keep my health benefits through January when I was finally scheduled to get my breast reconstruction. Best believe, I took my sweet time calling them back.

According to Anna Wintour, everyone needs to be fired at least once. It shifts how you think about work moving forward. Getting let go after nearly two decades felt like a load was lifted off my shoulders. I needed something to be the tipping point because I should've left long before. Similar to how Winston and I should have been over in our second year, I ought to have broken up with AT&T much earlier. I appreciate the company and what it did for me. It fulfilled a need in a different season of my life. As a single parent, I was reliant on my salary, and from that job, I provided a stable life for my kids. I had great experiences, from being in a sponsorship group, to traveling first class with the Warriors and watching them play, to the friendships I made. I loved it all. Still, I had a scarcity mindset back then. I was holding on out of fear, comfort, and complacency. Finally, after almost 20 years, I just stopped working and waited for the company to decide to let me go.

I was let go with five months left in my master's program. But it gave me space to pause and reflect. The biggest takeaway from my master's program was understanding my value system. My need for comfort, security, and familiarity is why I stayed at a job I did not like when I wasn't even passionate about the work. Or why I would let relationships linger until they were irreparable and wait for the man to break up with me. That same behavior was showing up for me in other aspects of my life. I didn't want to break up with people because I didn't want to hurt their feelings. I was afraid of what it would be like to be single or not to have a job. But I had to realize that what I was doing was holding me back. I didn't take many risks regarding my career. How many opportunities was I losing by not leaving the company? I was too afraid to take things into my control and get out of my comfort zone. I was letting life happen to me instead of asserting myself into it with intention. I had to get honest with myself that fear was at the root of many of my decisions, and comfort kept me stagnant.

That experience made me decide, if I was going to be on my Ps and Qs for the next job, then I needed to enjoy it. Period. It's hard to bring and be your best self when you hate going to work, which is what that event taught me. I can manage being fired because I know I will get another job. These companies always want us to think that we need to be happy that we have these positions. We're conditioned to believe that a paycheck every two weeks automatically equates to safety and security. But at the end of the day, we're all dispensable. It doesn't matter how much you're killing it in your position or how long you've been with the organization.

Instead of believing that we have to be a slave to a job, what it should be about is, 'I really love this role, and I think I bring a lot of value to the company.' So, no matter what, always choose you. Follow your passion, and be inspired. Period. Make the first move and create opportunities instead of waiting for life to happen. Trust and bet on yourself. You will thrive and be so much better for it. Opportunities abound – they're abundant and endless. You just have to believe in yourself and know you are worthy of going after it.

CHAPTER 9

Liberation is Liberating

By the time I left California for South Africa, I was already at peace about my time at AT&T coming to an end. The job wasn't for me and hadn't been for years. Still, I wasn't bold enough to make the first move and cut the cord. And the universe knew it. It was as if God was like, *girl, I guess I got to step in and make this happen because you won't get out of there.* I decided to let the chips fall where they may with no hesitation. Why let that get me down when I was living my best life in South Africa? My trip was already planned and paid for. So I wasn't giving AT&T another thought, except that they would just have to wait until I got home to make my termination official.

Gone for nearly two weeks, I went to Johannesburg, Karongwe Game Reserve, and Cape Town. I spent days exploring and pampering myself with incredible meals. While in Cape Town, I visited Table Mountain, where I rode the cable car up to its peak and took in the sights of the Atlantic and Indian Oceans and the aerial view of the city below. I also went to South African wineries. As I sipped on wine, and let the notes dance on my tongue, I'd look out at the picturesque scene of lush greenery and mountainous terrain. I seriously contemplated moving there because, why not?

SECOND ACT

There was a freedom I'd never experienced before being in another country without a job. Even though I'd traveled plenty, I always did it on borrowed time. I had to fit my trips in based on my vacation schedule at work, or I was doing it around the kids and their track schedule. There was always some external parameter. But this was the first time I could go and stay away for however long I wanted. I didn't have to be at work. I wasn't required to show up anywhere. And I took full advantage of it.

Traveling, to me, is about growth and exposure. Immersing yourself in other cultures makes you much more worldly and has diverse points of reference. You remove yourself from what America wants us to believe about ourselves – that we are superior to the rest of the world. From what I've seen, Americans tend to believe that other cultures are lacking or not as advanced as we are. Through an international policy lens, it's as if other cultures can't survive without us stepping in. Yet when you leave the borders of this country, you realize alternative places have a rich history, pride, and unique customs. You get to experience something new and out of the ordinary. It broadens your mind and changes your perspective on life, and you find that the world is so much bigger than the confines of our day-to-day.

As women, traveling unlocks so much for us. It adds color and texture to our lives. When we become wives or partners, mothers or caretakers, or leaders at work, we often get consumed with everybody else's schedule and don't take time for ourselves. Traveling allows you to have a change of pace, a break from your routine. It's a way of self-care, for sure. I say it teaches you gratitude. There are individuals in differing countries that can teach us so much about appreciation, pride, and human kindness. I also believe traveling lends itself to overcoming the fear of moving outside your comfort zone, whether you're going somewhere alone or on a group trip with people you've never met. And through traveling, there's the chance you could meet someone who may change your life forever.

Tamicka James and I met while I was in South Africa. At the time, she was a high-level executive working for Genentech, the world's first American biotechnology company. Tamicka is the type of woman who's warm and full of knowledge. We'd go out to dinner and spend the night laughing and talking over a bottle or two of wine. Unlike what people would like us to believe about successful Black women, Tamicka was willing to share information with others. As we spent time together, it came up in conversation that I wasn't working, and I told her I was looking to get into an entirely new career. From my admission, she started educating me about the medical device industry. This field is somewhat foreign to most people; back then, it was to me too. As the name implies, a medical device is a type of tool used to diagnose or treat disease. Think of an ultrasound or an MRI machine. The medical device industry is a competitive space, with companies always looking to innovate and push the health space forward.

Tamika shared how lucrative and fulfilling working in medical device work is, but she offered a balanced perspective. She didn't hold back about how underrepresented Black women are in the field. Although I was open to a new opportunity, at Tamika's company, they required incoming employees to have experience. Unfortunately, Tamika couldn't just say, "Hey, Cheri, take a look at my company." Yet she extended an invitation for me to call her

SECOND ACT

whenever I had questions. In fact, she's a very dear friend to this day.

Thanks to Tamika, I started noticing mentions of the medical device industry. It becomes one of those things that you start thinking about and hearing more of after you're exposed to it. When I returned to the States, a girlfriend of mine, Pam, got a position with Medtronic, a global leader in medical technology that reaches millions of people worldwide. They focus on four major areas – cardiac and vascular, invasive therapies, restorative therapies, and diabetes. It had been about two or three months since I was laid off and I loved it, but my forever curious mind was intrigued. I gave Pam my resume and, unbeknownst to me, she forwarded it to some people at Medtronic, where a job in diabetes had come up.

I got a phone call from Medtronic two months before I graduated from St. Mary's. For this role, the recruiter explained that I'd be responsible for working with diabetes patients. Even though I still didn't know much about the medical device industry, I knew I had no desire to work with patients. That's not to say it wasn't a wonderful opportunity, but it wasn't the one for me then. People thought I was crazy to pass up a job at Medtronic. But I asked the universe to help guide me in considering the position, and it didn't feel right. I was focused on learning to trust myself and my decision-making at the time. I didn't want to accept the role out of fear, lack, or anxiousness about getting a job simply to have one. So I went with my intuition and passed on it.

But that wouldn't be the last time I'd hear from Medtronic. When I finished my dissertation, the same recruiter called back about another role. This one would have me in the operating room with surgeons as they did spinal surgery and used Medtronic devices. Say, for instance, you have a herniated disc, and you need surgery on your back. The surgeons will put screws in your pedicles to give you stability, and rods to create height to take pressure off the disc. In my position, I'd be in the operating room, bringing in the tools the surgeons needed to help them through the surgery. Another part of my role would be sales, which really caught my attention. It required that I help doctors and hospitals understand the clinical benefits of implants and therapies. For the training program, I'd fly across the country and visit different operating rooms to meet with various surgeons and learn about their approach to using the devices. The more I thought about it, getting to work with orthopedic surgeons and neurosurgeons during spinal surgery fascinated me. With my love for knowledge, I knew I'd be in the room with intelligent people, getting the chance to talk to them and understand how their minds worked. Plus, spinal surgery was something so far from anything I knew. It'd be a new challenge, and I was up for it.

"I'm in a master's program and finishing up my dissertation," I explained to the recruiter. "If the stars align, and the timing works out for your interview, then I'll know this is the role for me."

I'm a huge believer that everything is about destiny. I ended up doing a first-round interview over the phone, and the interviewers loved me. They moved me on to the next phase – an interview panel in Memphis.

My graduation from St. Mary's was held on Memorial Day weekend, and my interview was scheduled for that upcoming

SECOND ACT

Tuesday. Without missing a beat, I packed my bags and flew to Memphis, where I stayed for a couple of days.

Going through a series of interview rounds, I was confident and composed. I knew I had it in the bag. I had the best preparation I could've ever asked for ahead of that interview, and that was running for the school board. My final interview was panel style, where three candidates, including myself, spoke with two or three people from the company. They asked a ton of questions, but the deciding factor came down to this one: "Why are you better than the candidate sitting next to you?" Since I'd been a contender for the school board gig, I knew exactly how to answer that question with decorum. The way I was trained, you couldn't trash your opponent.

"The other candidates have amazing attributes, and I think they would be great choices," I began, "but I'm going to tell you why I would be the best fit for the job…"

I emphasized my maturity and ability to learn anything. The panelist would come back and dig into my lack of a medical background. The other candidates had their master's in public health administration or were pre-med. To turn it around, I leaned on my experience in technology to demonstrate my aptitude for understanding complexity. I also emphasized how not only did I go to school for two degrees, but I did it while raising two world-class athletic children.

I made the winning shot, so to speak, when the panel posed this question: "What is your level of confidence for getting this job, on a scale of one to 10?"

"Ten," I replied without hesitation.

The guy competing against me scuffed. He'd told the panel that his confidence level was a seven. After hearing my answer, he rebutted.

"You know, I think in our job, you have to have some humility to be coachable…"

Can you believe he was trying to throw shade on me?

But I wasn't backing down.

"Well, I don't get C's in class, and that's what a seven is," I rebutted. "Seventy percent is a C. I'm an A student. I'm a high achiever. I've raised two world-class athletes, and when they step to the line, they never think they're not going to win.

"So I understand what it takes to win," I continued. "I know what value I bring to this job. And based on that, I wouldn't waste your time or mine if I didn't think I was highly qualified to be successful in this position."

Slayed it!

Of the seven people interviewed in that pod, I was the only one hired. Beating the odds, I wasn't the prototype for who is typically seen as the ideal candidate for that job – young, white, male, and athletic. I was a middle-aged Black woman. To this day, one of the women on the panel says my answer was probably the best she's heard in her career of interviewing candidates. Honestly, I wouldn't have even said it had that gentleman not challenged me and tried to be rude. The funny thing is, we're friends now. He didn't get the job, but we laugh about it to this day. What the panel knew that I didn't was that you have to be confident to talk to orthopedic surgeons and neurosurgeons and get them to trust you. So they knew that I could handle it. It couldn't have been more perfect. And that started my career in medical devices.

For you, dear reader, don't ever play small. You have no idea when an opportunity will present itself - one that needs your confidence, your quirkiness, and your magic. After years of conserving my appearance at AT&T, I walked into that room with my head held high and my hair in its natural state, a lofty, curly-haired afro. My ask for you is to always be your genuine self and fight against shrinking yourself.

***

I hired my first life coach six months before graduating from my master's program. I knew of them from other people and heard folks rave about the transformation they experienced from working with one. I found mine when a girlfriend took me to another friend's house. A woman there shared that she worked with a personal coach named Margaret Pazant. The woman said Margaret was challenging, but she came away from their time together in a completely different space. I knew someone like that was exactly what I needed. I asked the woman for Margaret's phone number and called the next day. I was ready to have a different life experience, and boy, did I get it.

Margaret's coaching was based on her book, *Genius Lives Within: Accessing Our Birthright Power*. In nine sessions, she helps her clients understand how everything they need to live a satisfying life and be the person they've always desired is inside of them. The blocks we experience occur because of our self-doubt and negative self-talk. Still, working with Margaret wasn't going to be a walk in the park. Frankly, she gave me the accountability I needed. I'd been able to navigate life being mediocre. I'm an A student, but I never had to study hard. As a procrastinator, I got my stuff done, but if I was more consistent and did less stalling, I would've been stellar. At work, it had been easy for me to pull together a proposal quickly or look at customer data right before a meeting.

From my first call with Margaret, it was clear that she wouldn't hold anything back. She called me out right away on things I had historically been able to get away with. I showed up five minutes late to the call, and tried to talk my way around it like I'd done many times before. She wasn't having it. She told me her time was valuable, and I would not waste it. If I showed up late, I'd still have to pay for the session without the benefit of her coaching.

During our time together, we also explored my relationship with my parents, and how it was impacting me and my interactions with men. As I learned in my master's program, my value system was around familiarity and comfortability. I tolerated infidelity because it did not challenge my sense of security, something most of the men I dated provided. It also felt normal due to my father's behavior. My inclination to be an overachiever and always take on multiple projects simultaneously came from wanting validation from my mother. Although I've always been pretty confident, I was also a worrier, a trait I picked up from her. I was definitely an overthinker and struggled with analysis paralysis. Mom was also argumentative, which was another characteristic I picked up. I couldn't be wrong. I now understand that was a sign of me not trusting myself and using discernment to guide me. As a result, I would ask everyone's opinion about major moves and went over and over about what I should do. I'm sure I got on my friend's nerves!

From working with Margaret, it was as if I flipped a switch. My whole life changed. She helped me evolve into a person, independent of my parents and their influence. I coached with her for less than a year, but when I look back at old journals, I see the difference. She shifted the way I thought about everything. I could see how negative I was about myself. We're often so hard on ourselves, especially as high-achieving Black women. Margaret changed all that. In my embryonic state of coaching, I'd start by reminding myself to meditate and then write what I felt after meditation. I'd write things like:

I can keep my word – to myself and others. / I can do, be, and have whatever I say. / I can become a master of managing myself and my word. The more I control my thoughts and what I am thinking, I can access power. What would be the outcome if I manage what I think, what I say, and how I act based on what I say to myself and out loud?

The foundation of all power and passion comes from what we think. Thoughts create things. Words become our world. Our power comes from within, not externally. All the answers are there, we just have to tap into them.

All my needs are met. The perfect job, finances, health, and partner. I'm looking for a miracle. I expect the impossible. The sky is the limit to what I can have. Just believe and receive. I am worth it. I deserve it. I can have it.

Coming out of my time with Margaret completely made over my self-talk. *Oh, I am amazing. I really am. Who wouldn't think I was? And if someone doesn't, that's okay. But they can't tell me that I'm not.* And that's why I could walk into that interview with Medtronic thinking nothing but positive thoughts. At no point did I think, *I'm not going to get this job because I don't have the background.* Instead, I told myself, *these people would be foolish not to hire me! I bring so much value to this space.* Frankly, that's how every Black woman needs to think about herself.

For people interested in working with a coach, I suggest finding someone who can be a safe place and hold you accountable. You have to be stretched and challenged to grow. Invest your time with someone you can trust so you can be completely open with them.

Going through coaching inspired me to continue working on my inner being in various ways. I started looking at different spiritual practices. I've experimented with yoni eggs, shadow work, mirror work, numerology, 360 work, and metaphysics. My experimentation started around 2015 when Facebook was revving up into a place where you could find groups of women talking about all kinds of spiritual and personal development methods. I gravitated to women working on their womb space – the creative power center for birthing new ideas into the world – and femininity. There was a side of me that could be a bit competitive and defensive. Knowing that, I wanted to learn how to be softer. One woman I came across (and still follow to this day), Tiffany

SECOND ACT

Janay, often talked about using yoni eggs and crystals. Reading her posts, I started using both for healing and clearing my chakras. I even went on meditation and womb retreats. It's funny because, at that time, you'd rarely see an executive woman in those 'woo-woo' type of settings. I guess that was my curious nature and inner Berkeley hippie coming out.

When it comes to metaphysics and shadow work, you can easily go into a deep rabbit hole. In this space, two names you may hear of are Neville Goddard and Abraham Hicks. Neville Goddard speaks about the law of attraction – specifically, how your inner state and what you surround yourself with creates your external life. Abraham Hicks is known for powerful rampages that everything will work out. She challenges her followers to analyze what story they are telling themselves and teaches that nothing occurs by happenstance. Metaphysics has everything to do with how you are and how you think. It's why you attract the things and people that you do. Based on that principle, if you attract broken people, then there's an aspect of you that's broken.

I think of metaphysics as going through a rebirth. It's about doing the inner work on yourself and your subconscious and understanding how your state of consciousness attracts your light. That's a core part of the training. You make the psychological shift from where you are to where you want to be. And that requires knowing who you are. This is where shadow work comes in. We suppress so much inside ourselves, whether it's because we had a bad childhood or we're embarrassed by something someone's told us. Whatever it is. My confidence is valuable to me, but I'd always felt like I had to contain it or people wouldn't like me.

From tapping into who I am and what I need in life, I was fully able to divorce myself from what others thought.

Tiffany always had interesting people in her Facebook group. From there I met a woman who did some numerology reading for me and another who coached me through 360 work. Three-sixty work is about making peace with your past, especially your interpersonal relationships. The exercises help you to recognize the value in a relationship, regardless of if it fails or not. Recognizing their benefits helps you to make peace with them. I had to reflect on and answer questions like, what was the beauty in that relationship? What was the challenge in them? What was my role in their demise? Whether we like to admit it or not, we all have our roles. When we start being more accountable, we can look at the relationship holistically, not just from one perspective. The goal is to heal from former relationships, so we don't take that bitterness into the next one.

When I think about my ex-husband, he gave me two remarkable children. But I saw all the red flags and moved forward anyway. I don't condone abuse, but I was definitely an active participant in the failure of my marriage. Ultimately, I had to release the resentment and sense of failure I had from the breakdown of our marriage. It was a learning experience. Moving forward, I know I won't make those same mistakes.

With Winston, our relationship had long run its course; yet, like with AT&T, I couldn't bring myself to call it quits for good. At his core, Winston was a great person. He always helped me out legally and financially. I think he loved me, but he was torn. After my

SECOND ACT

mastectomy, we did a few sessions in couple's therapy. I learned a lot about him during that time, notably how he lacked trust for women because of the infidelity he saw growing up. Though he was very well put together, with education and a successful career, like all of us, he wanted people to like him. I don't know for sure, but I suspect his physical appearance also impacted his self-esteem. He wanted to fit in with the cool kids, and since his friends didn't like me, he treated me like a secret. Today, I would never entertain a man who wouldn't be proud to have me on his arm. But I accepted that from Winston. Ultimately, I learned that he wasn't going to be completely honest with me. There was a limit to how vulnerable he'd be. And that wasn't going to lend to us having the intimate and emotional connection needed for long term success.

Counseling helped me to know more about who Winston was, but it didn't help us as a couple. It weakened us. But we didn't end it right then. The final straw came about three years later, before graduating from St. Mary's and getting hired at Medtronic. I knew he was continuing to date other people, and I was frustrated with his dishonesty. Instead of just letting it go, I tried to catch him on different occasions. One evening, Winston came to my house, and I started an argument. I don't recall what it was about, but it wasn't like I needed a valid reason. He was trying to leave, but I wasn't letting him. It was always extremely dramatic - sometimes, I'd stand behind his car or in front of his door. I had to prove my point and make sure he knew he was wrong.

"You're not leaving until we get to the bottom of this," was my infamous declaration.

Finally, Winston left.

And that was it.

Yeah, this is over. I finally got that out of my system. Ten years of being entangled in an unhealthy relationship. We were going nowhere, and it turns out he had already been dating someone else by the time we split.

When I think back on our time together, most of our issues could've been solved with healthy communication, addressing things head on, and not being afraid to "rock the boat" out of fear it would end the relationship (how many of us are guilty of that?). With Winston, it was as if I was a teenager again. Since he was a lawyer, I couldn't argue my point against him – similarly to how I felt talking about religion with my mother. She did not care how I felt. Conversation was not going to help our cause because he was going to be right, and again, my feelings didn't matter. I wish that time would've been different, but ultimately, it was crucial in my growth journey.

To give myself peace about Winston, I remember the benefits. He was exceptional to my girls and me financially. I was able to attend all of their international meets with no issues while they were growing up. It's something I appreciate, as I know life could have been different had he not been an integral part of it. He was a great friend, gave wonderful advice, and we had interesting conversations about almost anything. Yes, he had his issues, and I knew his faults, but it takes two to tango. I also played a part. I should've been much quicker to cut the relationship because we were better off as friends.

Today, I'm a firm believer in women being accountable for the role they play in relationships. It's not about what the man or the daddy did. It's about you and what you allow from the other person. When women share with me how they tell men not to "string me along," I quickly remind them it's not the man stringing them along; they are doing it to themselves. You have the power to walk away from any relationship that does not bring you complete fulfillment. Men can only treat you how you allow them to. It's never about the external. It's about how you feel about yourself internally and what you allow to come into your life.

***

From all my spiritual exploration, I've taken what resonates with me and made it a part of my lifestyle. Positive self-talk is non-negotiable. And when something bad happens, I take a step back and assess it. *Okay, how did I attract that?* I still follow the law of attraction and understand how my thoughts turn into things and my words into reality. Meditation is a part of my daily ritual, which Margaret introduced to me so that I could learn how to slow my mind and shift my thoughts from scarcity to abundance.

If you're interested in starting your spiritual journey, I suggest beginning with meditation. Learn to quiet your mind to stop the flow of all the chatter, the clutter, and the external things. Don't turn anything on when you wake up first thing in the morning. Don't look at social media. Instead meditate and visualize your day. Imagine how your day is going to be phenomenal and productive. Try your hardest not to let anything disrupt this sacred time. And while you're going to have contrast throughout the day, you have the tools to navigate it. Everything is about how you react. For example, if someone cuts you off in traffic, you don't have to cuss them out and give them the finger. All that energy is negative. You can reframe this by thinking, *wow, they must be late for work. I'm so happy that I saw them and was able to move accordingly.* That way, you can forgive them. Your whole perspective shifts by leaning into what feels good. And it all starts with the mind and how we begin our day.

When most people hear the word 'investment,' they automatically think about stock or real estate. But the best investment you can make is in yourself. Each time I did, whether it was my master's program, working with Margaret, or exploring spirituality and sexuality, the return I received was unlike anything I could've imagined. My life expanded tremendously. My relationships got deeper and more meaningful. My career accelerated. And my dating life got more exciting and healthy. But I promise you that nothing will change your life more than when you choose to invest in yourself.

CHAPTER 10

Believers Keep On Believin'

I once listened to an interview where Will Smith talked about going skydiving in Dubai. He describes his experience as "a confrontation with fear." He starts by detailing the hours leading up to the day, each more nerve-wracking than the one before. Finally, he's on the plane, bracing for the moment he's going to jump. As his toes touch the edge of the aircraft, he looks through the open door and down at the earth below. The countdown starts.

"One."

"Two."

On two, he's pushed off the plane and starts falling through the sky. "Ahhhhhh!" He says, illustrating the initial shock of free falling.

After being in the air for what he says felt like "one second," he realized something. He was having the most blissful experience of his life. "You're flying!" He exclaimed, reenacting how he weaved through the air, with both arms shaking and extended wide and a forced smile on his face. The experience led him to reflect and wonder – during that time he prepared to skydive. So what was the point of being afraid?

"It only ruins your day," he told the audience.

And then he said something that resonated with me.

"God placed the best things in life on the other side of terror. On the other side of your maximum fear are all the best things in life."

Having bungee jumped from Kawarau Bridge Bungy in New Zealand in May 2019, Will's story was one I could relate to. After my cancer diagnosis, I wasn't going to allow fear to dictate my life any longer. No more playing small. There was (and still is) greatness in the world, and I had to go get it. Changing your life truly starts with one decision. There was still plenty of work ahead that I had to do, but I was committed to doing it. Focusing on my personal development pushed me to dig deep and get honest about what I really wanted out of life. And that required having to step out of my comfort zone to try new things and experiences.

Continuing to feed my wanderlust was another promise I'd made to myself. The year following my double mastectomy, I went to Cuba and then Dubai. After going on that Mediterranean cruise in 2002 and visiting Morocco, I became intent on going to Africa every year. For the most part, I've followed through on that. I also based my travels around visiting the seven wonders of the world. I started in 2003 during my trip to Europe when I saw my first wonder, The Colosseum in Rome. The following year, I went to Brazil and checked off a second wonder from my list: Christ the Redeemer. In March 2017, I went on a mission trip to Peru with Aspire, Medtronic's women's employee resource group. We served the community by volunteering at an orphanage and teaching students English. We also got to visit some of the best restaurants in the world and hike Machu Picchu. About 17 months later, I went to Beijing, where I toured the Great Wall of China and had the best versions of Chinese food. For Thanksgiving 2019, Julian, Ashton, and I had a mother/daughter girls' vacation in Tulum, Mexico. We saw the Chichén Itzá, went to Casa Malca, Pablo Escobar's Mansion-turned-hotel, and enjoyed beautiful Cenotes.

But the two weeks spent in Egypt, Jordan, and Israel were unlike any trip I'd done before. A woman whom I traveled with before organized a group trip to Egypt, which Naimah and I signed up for. I couldn't miss the chance to go, especially when I'd get to visit the Pyramids of Giza (and my third wonder). The pictures simply do not do them justice. We often hear how we, as Black people, are not good at math and science. Yet, it took geometry and complex formulas to construct, what I believe, to be the most wonderful wonder of the world. Seeing the pyramids up close, I thought about how they stood for excellence and mastery and spoke to who we are as Black people—kings and queens with intellect and aesthetic prowess.

Besides viewing the pyramids, our group did a cruise along the Nile River. We also journeyed in a hot air balloon ride over the Valley of the Kings, a royal burial ground for pharaohs who ruled the country between 1539 and 1075 BC. There are said to be over 60 tombs there, but the public can see only a few. The view of the valley was majestic as we started the ride before dawn and saw the sunrise. When we ascended into the sky, I felt a gentle calm come over me as if I were wrapped up in a plush blanket. From the basket, which was much bigger than I thought it would be, we saw panoramic views of archaeological sites, monuments, crops, and even local farmers.

But as we floated over the valley, our balloon ran out of gas. We started falling from the sky, and that tranquil feeling I had earlier was instantly replaced with fear. But for some reason, I didn't think we were going to die. Even as we were dropping from the sky, it didn't feel like it was my time. I couldn't be on another continent, immersing myself in the history of our royalty and then have an accidental death. No way.

Outside of my head, the whole incident happened so fast. It wasn't long until we hit a tree, which stopped the momentum of our fall. Thankfully, no one had any injuries. And believe it or not, even with such a terrifying experience, I have no reservations about going on a hot air balloon ride again to this day. Allowing the thought of what 'coulda' happened or what 'could' happen if I were to do it again isn't useful. Instead, I think about the vow I made to myself, and try not to let fear win me over.

With Jordan and Israel practically next door to Egypt, I couldn't be that close and miss out on seeing places like the Rose City of Petra (another of the seven wonders), the Holy City of Jerusalem, and Tel Aviv in Israel. It's another fantastic city that gives you the best of both worlds – exquisite beaches along the Mediterranean coast and the vibrancy of a modern, multicultural city. You'll often hear it being referred to as "the city that never stops." Despite my own challenges with organized religion, it wasn't lost on me that those who identify as Jewish, Muslim, or Christian often want to visit those historic and holy sites at some point in their lives. I still appreciate and recognize the value of those devout activities. Adding in my infatuation with history, I imagined how culturally rich it would be to experience the

SECOND ACT

places we read of in the Bible and learned about to some extent in school.

For years I dealt with resentment about religion. I struggled with the concept that there was only one way to praise God, especially after seeing separate viewpoints. There was my mother and her commitment to Jehovah, Grandma Lillie and her devotion to the Holiness faith, and living on an Indian reservation with Momma Opal and Daddy Matthew. I was privy to how the community honored the sun, moon, and stars. It made me wonder why nature wasn't more integrated into religious practices. I also believe, as Black people, we have a complicated history with religion – Christianity specifically. Although the Christian Bible was used to manipulate enslaved people, we take so much pride in worshiping the same God that was pushed on us. Still, during the Civil Rights Movement, churches were our solitude. It's where we gathered to organize and refill our cups before going back out into the world to march for our freedoms. Those buildings stood as a symbol of hope. For me, it's all so complex. So instead of relying on a physical place to go or assigning myself to a denomination, I identify more with having a spiritual connection with the universe. But that's not to say I don't respect what people believe. I can embrace, respect, and honor all of it.

Ultimately, religion has had more impact on my life than I thought. It's played a role in developing my character, particularly my loyalty and integrity. I was reminded of that as I explored Jordan and Israel. Seeing where Jesus was born and baptized, it was as if I could feel his spirit throughout my body, and it filled me with gratitude. Standing at or near monumental spots in Abramhamic religious lore, places like the Dead Sea, the Wailing Wall, and the Dome of the Rock – all those things were inspiring to me. In those moments, I felt a profound attachment to God and walked away with a peacefulness that I still live with. I'd soon realize how such a transformational journey was symbolic of my evolution and a precursor for the physical transition I'd soon take.

***

I took a leap of faith to work at Medtronic. It was a new career in a different industry forcing me to take risks and make myself uncomfortable. Doing this required learning new clinical skills and subject matter, including anatomy, physiology, and disease states. Going into that job in my mid-40s, I didn't worry about my capacity to pick up new things. I'd just finished my master's program and was still in learning mode. Though I felt prepared for the moment, I sometimes felt the pressure. Making major career changes in that season of my life was not common, to say the least. Not only did I need to study and get up to speed, but there were still tests to take and pass. I was not immune from the uneasiness of being in an unfamiliar field. I was unlike the typical spine rep. As a mature woman among white males, often recent college graduates and former jocks, I was on the opposite end of the spectrum. When many of my colleagues would go out to drink, I didn't join them. Instead, I stayed in and studied. In this new environment, I certainly felt insecure at times. What kept me going was the trust and confidence I had in myself. Although I was stepping outside of my comfort zone, I would put my all into the job. This time, though, I wasn't doing it out of desperation or survival as I had done in my previous career. I loved the job and embraced

SECOND ACT

the opportunities I started getting access to. Overcoming cancer leaves you intent on finding things you can be passionate about. And that passion carried me through those times I had some self-doubt.

Over time, I'd find people who kept me confident and reassured me that I had the skills and ability to do the job. There was one gentleman, Mark – young, intelligent, and disciplined. He was the only Black man (and other Black person) in my class. He was also one of the few Black men in our role and in the industry. In that regard, we were some elusive unicorns. Though Mark could better fit the recent college grad and jock profile than I, he was still Black in a white space. We confided in each other often. Then there was my trainer, Phil, who noticed my talent. One of the managers I reported to, Hugh, was very supportive of me. Ultimately, I found the people who helped me navigate the two months of intense training required for new hires. And as we so often do in a predominately white space, the few Black people who were at Medtronic kept our eyes open for one another. Eventually, I started to make friends with other colleagues who looked like me.

The best part of my job was traveling up to 80 percent of the time. It satisfied my curious nature, and traveling the country was refreshing. After ending my on-again-off-again relationship with Winston, spending time alone was therapeutic. About a year into working at Medtronic, I received an offer that literally changed my life. Not only was I getting a promotion, but my new role would take me from California to Philadelphia. I would've immediately dismissed the idea if someone asked me years before. I never thought I would leave California. However, after my graduate school experience, I was aware of my need for security and actively wanted to challenge that. In one of my courses, we had to evaluate the opportunity costs of not taking risks. When I calculated the costs of staying comfortable, I realized I'd done myself a disservice for far too long. There were moves I could've made. I thought about moving to Atlanta when Julian and Ashton were young, but I didn't. I thought about how I could've been a homeowner years before I did. Ultimately, things always end up how they are meant to. Yet that shouldn't be used as a reason not to step out of our comfort zone.

Of course, I had my supporters and my naysayers. There will always be someone who's going to project their fears onto you. At the time, I was 45, and one of the warnings I got was that it would be hard for me to create a social circle as a middle-aged person in a new place. Being a west coast girl all my life, I'd heard of the cultural differences between the east and west. And the stereotypes about people who lived on the east coast—how they're rude and unfriendly. But there were also people like Naimah, who told me, "Girl, go, go, go!"

There's a mindset shift that needs to happen to take a bold jump. By working on myself, investing in coaching and exploring my spirituality, I've learned that we truly underestimate how powerful we are. It gets buried underneath all the external stuff we cross paths with throughout life. And it impacts who we are, whether it's something like growing up without a parent or having someone insult our appearance. Those things could make us less confident or cause us to start quieting ourselves. But when we reconnect with the internal, that's when we tap into our genius. That's where all the confidence comes from.

150

I also prepared for my move through meditation and visualization exercises. I'd think about moving to Philadelphia. I'd picture myself on the East Coast, spending time with friends. They didn't have faces, but there was an energy I felt. Using the power of manifestation, I had to feel like I was already living in Philly for me to believe it. In my mind, I was creating my new reality. Before I left for Egypt, I was a resident of Oakland. When I came back, I became a resident of Philadelphia. By the time I transitioned, I'd gone through a metamorphosis as far as having the mental strength around what my life could look like. And I created it.

***

As Black women, we deal with many obstacles in environments that weren't designed for us to succeed. Unfortunately, working in corporate often makes us question our worth and abilities. Usually, it has nothing to do with us and is more about the other person's insecurities. Everybody's at a different place in their career; some are the type to keep their head down and not rock the boat. I'm the 'push the envelope' type of person, and not everyone takes well to that. The medical device industry is a good ol' boys' network. When the harassment started, it showed me how some people prefer that you stay small, particularly as a Black woman. They'd rather do that instead of understanding how to coach the greatness that is you. One person, Brooke Story, was a mentor to me then (and still is today). She'd say to me, "Always be who you are, 100 percent. Don't ever dim your light."

Microaggressions start to wear on you as they build up over time. I remember when I was in Memphis with a group for training.

One night, we were discussing where to go for dinner. I can't recall if a choice was already made, or if we were still in the process of deciding. Regardless, I spoke up and suggested an alternative place to eat. "I think the food is better over there," I said. From that one comment, my female colleague tried to label me as aggressive. Just like that, someone can take something as innocent as offering another restaurant choice and try to accuse me of being hostile. There was another time when one of my colleagues, I'll call him Jake, asked me how it felt to live in Oakland, implying that I lived in the ghetto somewhere. When you are on the receiving end of a microaggression, it's all about reading between the lines. What this man was saying was, "You're Black, and I'm curious what that life feels like." In cases like this, it's not important for someone to know about where I live based on whatever idea they have about my home. Not only did I field comments like these from colleagues, but at hospitals, people thought that I was the orderly or the cell saver rep. No one ever thought I was the spine rep, and people regularly questioned my abilities.

No matter how outstanding my performance was in professional spaces, I still dealt with folks who couldn't 'manage' me. One of my bosses, I'll call him Tanner, was totally challenged by me. He'd tell me that I was "difficult to manage." *You don't have to manage me because I'm out in the field supporting my surgeons,* I'd think to myself. Still, despite other people's insecurities, I had to do my own reflection. Similar to my graduate program and working at AT&T, I had to remind myself that my confidence can be challenging to others. It's a delicate balancing act, for sure. Don't make yourself small, but it's also important to be mindful of how others receive you. I had to offset my confidence with a certain finesse that let

SECOND ACT

people feel comfortable around me. Otherwise, folks would be on edge or defensive with me almost immediately.

In a predominately white male space, we, as Black people, have to adapt so we can be successful in such an environment. Around this time, outside of work, I started leaning into my feminine space. I had to learn how to communicate to get what I needed. Dealing with all those men, I'd say things like, "I can see how you would say that," as opposed to, "What? No, that's not like that." Whatever the case was, I'd over-articulate. Even if they were completely wrong. It taught me a lot about how to connect in a different way than I'd done before. I learned I had the maturity to evolve and be strategic about it because I needed people to support me. I needed a band of cheerleaders. I needed people to think positively of me so that I could not only survive but succeed.

Although I loved my job and Medtronic, the bullying and mistreatment by certain individuals became too much. Remembering the promise I made to myself after cancer – to not deal with anything I didn't want to – I was willing to walk away from the job. Being open to new opportunities, my friend, Jay Vereen, presented me with a job referral to Zimmer Biomet. Zimmer Biomet is a medical device company that offers musculoskeletal health solutions. They had an opening for a regional sales manager. But when I looked over the job description, I hesitated. I was still new to the industry then and hadn't managed a region, people or product. I had a territory but wasn't responsible for revenue and driving it. I didn't believe I was qualified for the job. That is until one woman and one conference changed my mind. Mika Brzezinski, co-host of *Morning Joe*, hosted a women's conference

153

I attended. The theme was about worthiness, and I remember Mika sharing her story about how she had many jobs where she was underpaid. We also discussed how women only apply for jobs when they meet most, if not all, qualifications. Yet in comparison, men will apply just by meeting 60 percent. With that figure in my head, I shook off my uncertainty.

You know what? Let me test this out.

Although I didn't feel qualified, I applied. I wasn't going to let the 30 or 40 percent that I didn't have, stop me from putting my name in for the job.

Before interviewing with Zimmer, I decided I wouldn't alter who I was to make the interviewees feel more comfortable with me. And that included not changing my hair. For so long, Black women in the workplace have been conditioned to straighten or press their hair so they don't look too daunting or threatening. I went to my Medtronic interview with natural hair, so I no longer vacillated over if I should leave it alone or straighten it. When I walked through that door at Zimmer, I wanted to make sure that those people knew up front what they were getting. I went through several rounds of interviews. The first was with the recruiter. The second was with my future boss. Finally, the last was a group discussion, which three men sat in on – my soon-to-be manager, his general manager, and the founder of the division I'd be working in. Of course, I'd gone above and beyond in my preparation, studying the market, and putting together a PowerPoint presentation because as high achievers, that's what we do.

What was important to me was that I went as my authentic self so they could see me in my full regalia and glory. They needed to understand that 'she' was going to be the person who'd drive their business and ultimately go on to manage $90 million in revenue. Yes, the middle-aged Black woman with the 'fro. If they were in any way, shape, or form intimidated by that, then they had the option not to hire me. But they chose to. None of those men, at any point, felt as if they had to micromanage, cut me down, or feel attacked if I disagreed with them, asked a question, or helped them to think differently. They were secure in themselves and trusted whom they hired. When you bring your true self to the table, it's when you're most comfortable. That's why it's so important to embrace who you are. I also had to realize that the best working relationships I have are with people who are also self-assured. So, finding a work culture that meets your needs and values is possible. Instead of forcing yourself to fit in a box not aligned with you, find the one that's meant for you.

***

After Winston, I needed to shift my relationship with myself before getting involved seriously with someone else again. When I looked back on our time together, I thought less of him and more about me. Why did I let him treat me the way that he did? Many of us try to deny it, but our relationships are a mirror image of how we feel about ourselves. People treat us how we treat ourselves. And I had to get real about having a much better relationship with myself. Choosing celibacy was part of that. I wanted to eliminate any distractions from the work that I needed to do and get comfortable with being on my own. And I enjoyed it. Traveling for work, I'd do things like go out to a bar in New York alone. You tend to attract plenty of conversations and meet many people because folks are intrigued that you're out by yourself. I think so often, we as women feel like we need to be in a relationship because we're afraid to be alone. Today, I'm a big proponent of women learning to be content with being by themselves. If you don't like being alone, you don't like yourself. If you need to be around people at all times, or always try to bury yourself in another relationship, you've got some things to work on. I believe celibacy and time alone help you get to the root of a lot of that.

Around 2015 and 2016, I started seeking out relationship coaches. The first I came across was Pat Allen. She's what some may call an old school relationship coach, the original OG. I have a girlfriend who got married following Pat's teachings. From her, we learned about rotational dating, where you don't see one person exclusively but go out with several people. When I was celibate, I still dated, but Pat taught me how to converse with men differently. For the first time, I began to communicate that I was not dating exclusively confidently. Far too often, I don't think we define what dating is or have clear discussions about our status and expectations. We can still go out, have fun, and interact with other men. It's just a matter of, are we going to let somebody into our temple? Are we going to let someone have that intimate access to us? I believe that's the difference. Quite frankly, many men do not deserve nor have earned the right to have access to us in that way. Celibacy, I believe, provides some clarity around that.

Dating meant I had to get clear about my boundaries and have transparent conversations. To do that, I had to work on being clear with myself first and then others. If you don't have a powerful relationship with yourself, then it's hard to have a confident, vulnerable, and honest connection with anyone else. So I started saying what I wanted upfront. For instance, I'd say, "Are you okay with just dating? And I mean without intimacy, because I want the next man I'm intimate with to be my husband." This is the type of communication that I see lacking in relationships. Then I started developing conversations with men who had similar values and were aligned with the things that I wanted out of life. Whenever I'm asked about growth in communication skills, I suggest a book I was required to read in my master's program called *Nonviolent Communication: Life-Changing Tools for Healthy Relationships* by Marshall B. Rosenberg. It talks about how to articulate what you're feeling, so it's more palatable to the other person instead of framing the conversation in a way that puts the other person on the defensive.

As I was establishing myself in Philadelphia and looking for a social circle, I tried different social activities. Through one social site, Meetup.com, I found a group for Black women who hike. It was during one of their events that I met a young woman. We talked during the hike, and I told her I was new to the city. By then, I'd been in the city for about two months. We exchanged numbers, and about a week later, she called me.

"I want you to meet someone."

She sent me a picture of a handsome man named Jimmie. He had a shaven bald head that accentuated his pristine dark skin. He wore glasses and had a beard sprinkled with salt and pepper hair. I told her I was down to meet him. A few nights later, he and I met and had dinner at a Black-owned French restaurant called

Paris Bistro & Jazz Cafe. While I was enjoying my cocktail, jumbo lump crab and avocado, red and gold beet salad, and red snapper, the conversation with Jimmie was flowing. He was interesting. We talked about my transition to Philadelphia, my career and my family. We really hit it off. I'd later find out that Jimmie was the young woman's father!

Standing between 5'11 and 6 feet, Jimmie was near my parents' age group. He kept himself up pretty well by walking often. Jimmie was of average build and looked good for his age. He had unique clothes, which he accumulated from his travels. He had a smile that would light up a room and would smirk whenever he was amused. My attraction to him was because he partly reminded me of my dad. Jimmie walked with a confidence that gave off the sign that he was very sure of himself. Although he had a challenging background, he put himself through school and became a lawyer and a judge. I wasn't necessarily drawn to his success, but it was his poise, for sure.

Jimmie was my first relationship coming out of those two years of celibacy. With him, I had a much more mature and honest conversation about what I wanted early on. I explained that I wanted to be married and asked if that was something he was open to. At the time, he was. It was the beginning of a three-year relationship, which, by that point, was my healthiest and most honest relationship. To my knowledge, Jimmie never lied or was unfaithful to me.

But as time went on, I realized there were qualities I wanted in a partner that Jimmie didn't have. One area that we disagreed on was money. We had opposing viewpoints, and the way Jimmie handled money did not sit well with me. But nothing solidified the end for us more than the day we went to the wedding of a friend of mine, Keisha. It was the catalyst that helped me refine what I wanted from a partner.

Keisha and I met and worked together at Medtronic. During that time, she also met her future husband, Kevin. From the moment I met him, I could tell. "This is your guy," I told her. Keisha had dated good guys before, but they weren't her *guy*. I could tell from the way Kevin doted on her. I could see from the way he catered to her that he would be her spouse. And sure enough, he proposed. While I was super excited for them, I had no idea that being a guest at their wedding would forever change my own life.

The day before their wedding, Jimmie and I had an intense conversation. I'd been looking for some additional real estate to purchase, and we were going to invest in a property together. During the discussion, something he said stood out to me.

"Do you have your half for this deal?"

I was stunned by his question. With a firm tone, I replied, "I absolutely have my half for the deal because this is business, and I'm always going to be prepared when it comes to business."

It wasn't what he said but how he said it. And I knew the context behind it.

"I know how you think men should pay for everything," he responded as if that was an explanation for his initial question.

"This is different. It's business, and I've always had my portion of the investment to close the deal."

Jimmie was the type who, if there were a bill for twenty-five dollars, he would ask if you had twelve-fifty. A friend of his once told me that Jimmie's approach to money stemmed from growing up poor. What I've found is that for our people, being raised in those conditions can cause us to have a scarcity mindset. Growing up, not seeing anyone with significant wealth or watching our families and communities struggle can impact our money mindset. However, from my spiritual work, I've retrained myself to think about money as abundant. I believe that because money flows freely, we'll always have it.

By nature, Jimmie was a generous person. Though I believe some of his hesitations came from having women in past relationships who possibly took advantage of him. He'd also told me that my strength reminded me of his mom, which left him conflicted with me.

Still, our conversation about the investment property left a bad impression. That night, I went back to my place alone.

The next day, we went to the wedding together. Keisha and Kevin were married at the Philadelphia Museum in the Egyptian section. The museum holds one of the country's largest Egyptian and Nubian collections, spanning Egypt's history from circa 4000 BCE through the 7th century CE. Already honored to be at the event, my face beamed at the familiar sight of the pottery, jewelry and pieces of architecture on display. But more than the ambiance, it was the apparent love between Keisha and Kevin that left an impression on me. During the reception, I took note of how Kevin described Keisha as his reason why. When Keisha's father spoke, he talked about how he felt comfortable giving away his baby girl, whom he's very protective of, to Kevin. He said he knew Kevin would take care of her. It was then I realized what was missing between Jimmie and me. I didn't feel cherished and appreciated in the way that I wanted.

You could feel the energy shift between us after the wedding. And we both knew it. The silence spoke louder than any words could've after leaving the reception.

"Wow, that was something," he finally said.

I agreed. "Yeah, that was something."

Our conflicting attitudes about money were a hurdle too big for us to get over. And the wedding proved that I needed more. I wanted the type of devotion that Kevin had for and showed to Keisha. I cherished myself too much to think I could move forward with Jimmie. I needed to release him, but more importantly, myself.

The day after the wedding, I called him.

"I want to inspire a man the way Keisha inspires Kevin," I explained. "I want a man to take care of me the way Keisha's dad feels Kevin will take care of her. And that's not what you do. You're a great person, and I'm a great person, but I don't think I inspire you in the way I need my husband to."

Looking back on it, Jimmie preferred to be single. But since he wanted to be with me, he was open to exploring marriage. Still, as a lawyer, I'd hear how his mentees spoke about women. The group's perspective was, "If a woman steps to me, she's got to bring something to the table." Jimmie never spoke to me with that tone, but that was his point of view. I wouldn't say he walked through the door talking 50/50, but that was his mindset around money. And it showed. Those two years on my own gave me the confidence and self-love to be okay with walking away if Jimmie didn't want what I wanted. So I let him go, and it was the best thing I did for me.

So many people were surprised when Jimmie and I broke up. For all intents and purposes, we looked like a great couple. But we weren't. I had friends tell me, "Girl, it's rough out here. If that's your only issue, you can work that out," and "It's lonely. You don't know who you're going to get." All of those things would've made me stay for my old self. But not this time. I wanted to be cherished, but I couldn't get that from Jimmie. It was a tremendous test for me. Since nothing was wrong in the past, I wouldn't have approached a man about ending a relationship. I would've stayed and died a slow, painful death. This was proof that the work was working.

When taking risks in life, I believe in using passion as your guide. In your career, you have to be passionate about the work you do because you spend a lot of time doing it. And understand that when one door closes, another one opens. Figuratively, when my door closed at Medtronic, another one was ready for me to open up. It may not seem like it, but there's always something better

SECOND ACT

when you're having struggles at work or in relationships. Don't stay because you think you're going to be lonely or you won't find somebody else or another job. Don't hang around anywhere you are not honored, respected, cherished, or don't experience joy every day. Be confident that the door you're supposed to walk through will open for you. Have faith and trust that it will happen.

CHAPTER 11

The Golden Year

When searching for love, we often have that perfect list of our ideal partners. There's a full rundown of his physical features, income, assets, or the title that must appear next to his name. We can recite the list with our eyes closed. We know it like the back of our hands. Whenever a man approaches us, our brain starts calculating whether he's going to pass the test. *Does he check all the boxes?* But here's the thing – we can't attract the right guy based on a shopping list. There has to be more.

As Black women, we've grown accustomed to measuring our worth based on our accomplishments, and by extension, looking for those in a potential mate. Sure, accolades are great, but they say nothing about a man's character. We can even take it a step further. There's another piece of the puzzle that we often overlook. We're quick to construct the man of our dreams on paper, but we give less priority to becoming the woman of his. We skip over the part where we need to focus on healing past traumas or overcoming limiting perspectives. We miss out on embracing periods of deep reflection, asking ourselves hard questions, and investing in being a better listener, communicator, partner, whatever that is. It's crucial to pause and design the life

SECOND ACT

and person we want to be before inviting someone else into our space.

Working on all our stuff, so to speak, is not always pretty. But real growth starts from an honest place. When I began coaching with Margaret in 2015, we cut right to the center of what was holding me back – my mindset and negative self-talk. Whenever I look back at my journals from that time, I can see my transformation scripted in black ink, line after line and page after page. We talked about the value of being present– through meditation– and taking seven minutes out of the day for breathing. We discussed how I was showing up in the world. And I didn't realize how small I was playing. I never felt comfortable being me. When you're not connected to yourself, it creates frustration and confusion. So I had to play out on paper what it would mean to play as my biggest self.

To do that, Margaret and I worked on using power statements. This type of thing may sound woo-woo to some, but affirmations do play a role in changing our mindset. In my journal, I wrote declarations like these:

I am optimistic and confident in all that I do.

I am the creator of my life and my world.

I fill my mind with positive, nurturing, and healing thoughts.

Everything always works out for my highest good.

I was serious about transforming my life and had to write about what I wanted in detail and with intention. I got very specific

165

about the areas I wanted to grow in my career, life, and love. By calling out my weaknesses in my journal, I gave myself a roadmap for how I wanted to evolve:

I can still be a bit offensive, off-putting and judgmental of others' journeys, which can show up in my responses to people. My words are not as eloquent as I would like them to be.

I want to speak confidently and with grace when I speak my truth and ask for my worth in compensation. I don't want to be nervous and unsure. I want to be at ease.

I want to work on being warm and soft so that my strength is not diminished but that I am not intimidating.

When I talk about describing a man's character, I had to do the same for myself first. This is how I uncovered the best version of myself – the healed, complete, and genuinely happy Cheri. As I became clearer about who I was, I started preparing my mind and heart for my future husband. I wrote how I deserved to receive massive amounts of affection every moment of every day and expressed to the universe that I was open for love. I thought about my goals, one of which was wanting a passionate, deeply fulfilling, supportive relationship. One exercise I did was write down five things of value I bring to a relationship and another five areas I believed I could improve in.

I am interested in life

I am not judgmental

I set goals

I don't compete with my husband

This helped me to look at myself objectively to bring positive things into my life. When you want to attract your mate, it goes much deeper than how he looks or what he has or can do. I had to get specific and ask myself what type of man fit into my life:

Is he a man I can respect?

Does he recognize his purpose and potential?

Is he a man of his word? Does he follow through?

Is he someone who will support me in my growth?

I thought about what I considered to be the foundation of a good relationship and how I wanted to feel in that partnership:

A king who takes care of himself can take care of you. If you don't allow a king to take care of himself, then he can't take care of you

I want to feel sexually satisfied

I want to feel adored

I want to feel smart

I was serious about finding my husband, and I knew he was out there. From listening to Abraham Hicks, I knew I had to speak about him as if I already had him. When I was ready to describe my husband, I listed not his accolades, but his personality.

I want to find the man of my dreams. I want the man of my dreams to find me. I want him to have the following characteristics:

Honesty

Loyalty

Spirituality

Confidence

Loves to travel

Wants to make the community better

A good person with integrity

Great sense of humor

Like a chill in the air that whispers the seasons are changing, I was yearning for something different as I approached my 50th year. At that point in my life, I hadn't gotten into a man's heart. I knew I wouldn't get the result I wanted by continuing to date with the same strategy as before. Instead, I wanted to attract a quality companion and learn how to speak to his core. And that required a shift. When you're ready for change, the universe tends to show out, revealing people and opportunities in your path.

After learning about rotational dating from Pat Allen, I adopted another concept she taught – masculine versus feminine energy. She'd explain that if you need to be the 'man' in the relationship, then you need to find one who's okay with that and takes on a more feminine role. I felt naturally feminine, but I knew I had masculine dynamics. Being raised by a single parent and becoming one, and working in an industry with majority white men, it was hard for me to switch from masculine tendencies to feminine

SECOND ACT

ones. One way this showed up was in my being the one to always take charge.

As I worked on my natural femininity, I found another relationship coach – April Mason. She's also known for her teachings on femininity, and online dating. Growing up in the Bay Area, I knew of it, but didn't feel the need to try it at the time. Back then, the stigma was that online dating was for Silicon Valley professionals who were too busy and socially awkward to date traditionally. You had to be desperate to be online or have something wrong with you. That belief stayed with me. Since I was out meeting people and having relationships, I saw no reason to be online. Because of April, though, I became more open to the possibility of using it.

***

The start of the year can feel like a time of renewal and anticipation. For some, it can gradually wind up before life starts to pick back up again. Twenty-twenty was the beginning of a new decade, and some folks predicted it would have that feel of the Roaring Twenties. It would also kick off a fresh decade for me— my golden years. I had a three-day bash to celebrate as I usually did for my birthday. And girl, let me tell you, it was a whole vibe! It started on Friday with a welcome celebration. My close friends from California flew out for the occasion, and they got the opportunity to meet my other friends in Philly. That night, we all went to eat at Vernick Fish. It's one of my favorite restaurants in the city, located on the floor level of the Four Seasons hotel. While there, I gifted each person with a picture of them and me, and talked about their significance in my life. After dinner, we went to a bar and restaurant at the top of the hotel, with the best view of Philadelphia, hands down! On that night, the L.A. Lakers were in town to play the 76ers, and I came face-to-face with Lebron James. I *love* him and said to myself earlier that I was going to meet him – talk about manifestation! Day two was supposed to be a tour of historical and Black Philadelphia, but a rainy day meant we had to cancel. Still, we ended the day in style with a catered birthday party in a beautiful city loft. There were custom craft cocktails, an ice sculpture, and a bomb DJ who had us dancing the night away.

I officially turned 50 on that Sunday, January 26. My friends and I had a catered brunch at a cozy venue, called The Gathering Place. During the event, we were treated to an unbelievable musical interlude by my friend Soloman, who sang along with a beautiful songstress named Hannah. But the day also seemed surreal. It was the same day that Kobe Bryant died. His passing was a reminder that life is not promised, and it's important to live fully, aim high, and love on your loved ones. I truly believe a scarcity mindset has no place in our lives. So spend the money. Have the experience. Do the thing that brings you joy!

Outside of my birthday weekend, work was calm. Typically, I traveled about 80 percent of the year. There's a lull in January for the medical device industry, particularly sales. There's a frenzy that happens in December. Deductibles have been met, so patients are getting elective surgery. At the beginning of the new year, deductibles are reset. We don't have quotas yet, so January feels like a hangover month for the industry. By the end of the month, though, we have a sales meeting that gets us all fired up and ready to go back into the field. By February, I was back to my normal travel schedule.

In early March, I was in Nashville when I got a call from my boss. He said the company started restricting travel, and this trip would be my last. *What's going on?!* I wondered. Watching the news from my hotel room, I saw reports of people getting sick from an upper respiratory disease called COVID-19. Of course, no one knew the severity of what that meant yet. I flew back to Philadelphia from Tennessee on Friday, March 13. After getting home, I went out to meet a friend at a gin distillery. I had no idea that would be the last time I'd go out socially for the foreseeable future.

As did much of the world, at my job, we went from seeing surgeons in person and sending reps out in the field for training to going virtual. Our pay was cut by 20 percent temporarily, which my employer said was to prevent layoffs since no one knew how long we'd be in quarantine. Going from traveling nearly three-fourths of my time to now zero was an unexpected blessing I didn't realize I needed. It was a gift that allowed me to take a step back and reflect. Traveling is great, but it's also busy. When you're getting on a plane, moving from one city to the next, living out of your suitcase, and then coming home and hitting the streets because you've been gone for so long – it really is a grind. Being on the go like that distracts you from being still and present. You don't have the space to let your mind recharge. But by staying put, I learned to be more efficient in my role and realized I could do much more with my teams.

Outside of work, COVID made me face the reality of what was missing in my life. I looked around my home. There I was in my two-bedroom duplex, alone. *What if I died in here? Who would come and get me?* Even though I had friends in Philly, we were all hunkered down. It wasn't like if I were home, quarantining with my people in California. I stayed connected with family and girlfriends through FaceTime and Zoom calls doing virtual happy hours. With each day that passed, the uncertainty about how long the shutdown would last was difficult to ignore. I remember the president claiming we'd be out of quarantine by Easter. I wished he was right. I would've flown home to California if his prediction had been accurate.

Since I wasn't traveling, I had a routine work schedule for the first time in a long while. I'd log on at 8 or 8:30 in the morning and end at 7:00 since I managed a team on the west coast. It differed from how I worked before COVID when I'd be online from 6 a.m. to 10 p.m. It was unfamiliar to me to have that much time. And without being able to go out socially, it gave me plenty of time to reflect. I was in a space to find love, and in a way, the pandemic created some urgency around that. Frankly, I didn't want to die alone. The thing about living through a pandemic and being in quarantine is that it heightened people's need for companionship. Jimmie was one of those people. He, like many others, didn't want to be alone in the pandemic, and rightfully so. Although he and I didn't align in certain areas, we didn't end the relationship on bad terms. He reached out to me and offered to do things like cook dinner for me and bring it to my house.

Jimmie wasn't the only man who cared for me during quarantine. After breaking up with Jimmie, I dated a guy for a short time named Reggie. He brought me groceries and checked on me. Like

Jimmie, he was a great person, kind and gentle, but not for me. While we were dating, Reggie worshiped me. I mean, he *loved* me. Unfortunately, Reggie was a big fish in his small pond, with minimal exposure to a world bigger than his block. When my 50th birthday weekend came, and all my powerhouse girlfriends from California were in the the room, he didn't know how to show up. He shrunk. He was uncomfortable, and it showed. Although Reggie made me feel so special, protected and provided for – all the things I loved – he lacked confidence in himself, which is a quality I needed from a man. From the time we spent together, Reggie showed me what it was like to be with a man who loves you more than you love him. And it feels like being honored, cherished, and respected. I walked away from that relationship knowing what it was that I wanted.

Being comfortable with Jimmie and Reggie, it would've been incredibly easy for me to give it a shot with either of them. Had this been the Cheri from a few years ago, she would've done that because she valued familiarity. I could've settled for either man out of fear of being lonely. But I chose not to go that route. We tend to block so many of our blessings by not having the confidence to be alone. How can your person come if you're distracted by someone else? Because I was so complete with myself, I was comfortable leaving men and relationships who were great but not *right*. You can't be with someone temporarily to fill a gap. In hindsight, all those decisions I made opened the door for the right man to enter my life. And he gave me what both of those men did and so much more.

***

Although those early perceptions of virtual dating stayed with me, I tossed them aside by March. Being at home, not dating anyone, I decided to go online. *Shoot. I'm not going to be in here by myself. Let me have some fun!* I thought the pandemic would only be a couple of months anyway. Then I'd be back out meeting people, traveling, and living my fabulous life. So, in the meantime, I was going to embrace the journey.

Being in sales and marketing, I had a strategy for setting up my dating profile (you might want to take some notes!). Being clear about the person I am, I wanted my confidence, joy, and inner peace to shine through the screen. I looked through my best pictures and asked myself, *what makes me look fun?* I lived a great life, and I wanted to portray it in that one-dimensional space. So I picked a picture of myself at Machu Picchu in Peru and one at a party dressed up, having a night on the town. I used one of myself hiking to show my active side. I selected others that showed me with no make-up , with my hair straightened, natural, and with a braided weave-in. In all, I had six or seven pictures, including a full-body shot. I wanted men to see all aspects of me: no selfies or bathroom shots.

For my caption, I could've easily just listed the facts – I'm from Oakland, I live in Philly, and I work in sales. But I took the opportunity to show my lively and playful personality.

A girl from the Bay, living in the City of Brotherly Love

You get the mood, vibe, and energy of the West Coast combined with the quick wit, pace and authenticity of the East Coast.

I'm a curious explorer, so there's not a plane going too far or a hole in the wall Speakeasy too small.

I am an extroverted introvert, so I do appreciate a good book, podcast, and binge-watch of Succession, Insecure, Power or Race for the White House. I also appreciate nature, so I am open to the occasional hike.

I travel 80% of the time for work, but I love trying new restaurants on the road, seeing sights and doing what tourists do in between meetings.

I wouldn't mind a partner in crime. If you want to do time with me, reach out.

I wanted my words to leap off the page, for men to think: *she's fun and I want to be in her life!* People pay attention to those things. Writing something like, 'I'ma try this one more time,' easily repels. You have to be in it to win it. Just as you would on a first date, act like the fly, beautiful, and worthy queen you are! Be comfortable with showing up as you, not your representative. Eventually, you're going to have to show your future companion who you are.

To me, being online is like looking for a job. You want to have a great resume to attract the best hiring manager. Your online profile is your resume. The time and intentionality you put into making sure that it shines can impact your virtual dating experience. So often, we give so much weight to our resume for a job or application for school. But we'll throw up anything as an online dating profile. It should be just as powerful and pristine as those other things. Similar to how work and school impact our lives, whoever comes into your personal space can shift the trajectory of your life. Not only that, but I genuinely believe it's all about your mindset. If you think you're going to have a bad experience, even subconsciously, then you will. All those things that tend to happen are self-fulfilling prophecies. You expect you won't have a good experience, so you don't put enough effort into it and have a bad one. And now you're left feeling that online dating is trash. But there are too many statistics and experiences that show otherwise.

Still, there are valid concerns about dating online. The first thing to know is there are many websites, so pick whatever's comfortable for you. Be confident and use discernment. Ask lots of questions. Don't take anything offline until you feel ready. And set boundaries upfront. I've heard of some people having a Google number. If that makes you more secure, do it. There are things you can put in place to protect yourself.

I had no expectations, except to enjoy myself. And I did. There were so many people in my inbox. My positive juju was attracting some hot ones! Outside of guys calling me a little too much, I didn't experience those horror stories of dick pics and ghosting. One day, I logged on to the site and found a new message from a man I hadn't connected with yet. His name was Tracey. In the note, he welcomed me to Philly. I took a closer look at his profile picture. This man was fine as could be. His ebony eyes beamed from behind a pair of glasses with dark frames. He had flawless chestnut skin; his hair was silver with sprinkles of black, short and lined up with rows of waves. A perfectly manicured goatee framed a smile radiating from the screen so much it made me tingle in all the right places.

His pictures made it apparent that he had style, dressed in tailored suits and newsboy caps. Assuredly knowing I can pull myself together, I replied to his message.

SECOND ACT

"Hey! We'd look good stepping in a room together."

From that first exchange, we kept the conversation going. It didn't take long for us to set up our first Zoom meeting, which we scheduled for early April.

When I tell you, I was jittery and had a tough time thinking about anything else! Normally, for a first date, you want to do it up. Maybe a manicure or get your hair done. Except in a pandemic, you're on your own. I hadn't done my hair in so long, because I was used to going to the salon and getting my natural tresses coiled up and looking cute. Well, I tried to recreate that and it. Did. Not. Work. When I turned my camera on to meet Tracey, I showed up in a voluminous afro.

Aaaaaaahhhh! I thought to myself. But I kept it cool mostly, although Tracey came on wearing a mask. It kind of scared me, but it also showed his fun, silly side. It certainly broke the ice between us. Once we were settled on video, we started talking like it was nothing. I was a bit self-conscious but Tracey, in his voice, sounding smooth as silk, kept saying, "You're just so beautiful." All I could think about was how confident and witty he was.

There was something about the way we engaged with each other that was light and refreshing. It was flirtatious, but in a very respectful manner. When we first met, using laughter to break the ice easily helped shake off the nerves. And I realized I liked him. So much so, I wanted to hear his voice as often as I could. Over the next few weeks, we connected over FaceTime calls and Zoom dates throughout the day. We had breakfast together, met for coffee, had dinner by candlelight and attended church.

We never ran out of things to talk about. Using Tracey's profile as a starting point, I'd ask questions to learn more about him. I stayed away from close-ended questions. People will be quick to say yes or no in an uncomfortable, awkward situation. But asking open-ended questions prompts them to share more and shows that you're taking an interest in them. For example, he said he was an instructor.

"Help me understand what you teach."

"Why did you get into what you're doing?"

"What inspires you about the work that you do?"

As handsome as Tracey is, he's also very deep. Our initial conversations were around advocacy, our passions, career choices, past relationships, and what we were looking for. We were really connected by the time we had our first date on May 22, 2020. We also were aligned about bringing attention to the issues that affect our community. Unfortunately, George Floyd was killed a week after our date. Wanting to push for a conversation about diversity at work, I talked with Tracey about how to best approach that. We'd also discuss the state of the healthcare system and how vulnerable we were as a community due to the pandemic.

The other thing with dating is that it's also about practicing. People feel like every person they meet has to be that one, so they lock in on them. And if they don't like someone, they won't engage with them. Many people I knew would not be my one, but I engaged with them. It helped me build up my communication skills, and granted me the ability to work on some things I felt I needed to improve. It was beneficial dating in a pandemic when the only thing you could do was talk. It's okay that a person isn't your ideal partner. Everyone can be an experience and add value to your life in some way (as long as they're not deranged and crazy!)

Tracey soon wanted to know what my intentions were – and I welcomed the conversation. Every man that I dated, I asked the same question – what would your ex say is the reason why you guys broke up? I wanted to know if the guy had any accountability and self-awareness around that. Of course, Tracey didn't tell me everything right away. Some things I found out later. But, for the time we knew each other, I thought he was pretty vulnerable and open with sharing. For Tracey, I think he was feeling good about me and sizing me up. I told Tracey I was dating for marriage, just as I had with the other men I interacted with. I explained that, for the men I met, I was dedicating my time to those who were marriage-minded first.

"Don't worry, that doesn't mean I'm desperate and it has to be you," I clarified. "If you're not marriage-minded, that's okay. You're really great, and we'll probably be friends. But I'm decidedly prioritizing men with that goal."

"Hey, me too!" He said eagerly. I know now that Tracey wasn't trying to get married. He's very much a relationship person, but at his age, 57, he didn't think he would have that experience again.

After about four weeks, we decided to move offline and have our first in-person date. Even though Tracey sent me that message welcoming me to Philly, he actually lived in Trenton, New Jersey. In May, New Jersey and Philly started relaxing some of their

COVID restrictions, and we set our date for the third week of the month. Tracey often said how he wished we could go to a restaurant together. Listening to that need, I attempted to create that experience. So I arranged for a restaurant-style dinner date at my home. I hired a friend of mine, who's also a chef, to cook a multicourse meal. I had menus created and place settings. We also had a violinist there to perform songs like Nat King Cole's "Unforgettable," Bobby Caldwell's "What You Won't Do For Love," and Michael Jackson's "Butterflies."

I had no reservations about inviting Tracey into my home. Since he and I spoke for weeks, I had a sense of who he was. I also have a strong intuition, but still play it safe. I've always dated professional men, so, if anything, they have something to lose. Plus, in all the places I've lived, I've had a form of protection. At my duplex, for example, my tenants were all men. And I'd let someone know when I had a date coming over.

That night with Tracey became one of my favorite dates with him. He couldn't get over what I put together and told me how "blown away" he was. It kicked off a vibrant summer of us spending more time together. On the 4th of July, we went away to D.C. for our first trip. You can tell how well you travel with someone when you go away. And for us, it was a perfect vacation. Another time we went to Asbury Park, New Jersey, where Tracey's from, and had a picnic on the beach. The shore there is charming and reminded me of Martha's Vineyard. In Tracey's 1979 Mercedes-Benz convertible, we'd cruise along the East Coast, having singalongs to classics like Bill Withers' "Ain't No Sunshine," The Brothers Johnson "Stomp," or some other R&B classic.

SECOND ACT

While I was upfront with Tracey about my intention for marriage, I tried not to push the issue anymore after. I wanted to take a more traditional stance and allow Tracey to lead. I'd done that in previous relationships, always trying to force the needle. I was always trying to dictate everything, even down to the proposal. But under the femininity teachings, the man is the pursuer. And I hadn't done a good job of letting them do that before. But with Tracey, I didn't really have to talk about it. Ultimately, I learned that I had so much more influence leaning back than I ever did trying to force and push something. That summer, Tracey asked me for exclusivity. A month after we met in person, he was already introducing me as his fiancée to his family and friends. Steve Harvey says a man who's into you will provide, protect, and profess. Well, Tracey was professing big time. He also spoke about us in very future terms. For instance, he'd talk about the house he wanted to build for us. All those things let me know that it wasn't just his word. It was his deed that we'd spend our lives together.

But if there's anything about Tracey, he would do it on his time. I thought he was going to propose for Christmas. But he didn't. Yes, I was leaning back, but my inquisitive disposition still got the best of me.

"Baby, is everything okay?" I asked slyly. "Are you having any concerns about our relationship?"

He was on to my game. "Nope."

For New Year's Eve, Tracey and I had plans to go to dinner and spend the night at the Four Seasons Hotel. We went to a well-known restaurant in New Jersey, called Rat's. At this point, since my birthday was less than a month away, and Valentine's Day would come about two weeks later, I figured Tracey was going to pick one of those days to make a move. He kept saying that 2021 was going to be our year. That should've been my first clue, but it went over my head. During dinner, he excused himself from the table to go to the bathroom. When he came back, I noticed he was a bit off from how he usually was. Now, Tracey is a super confident and very smooth man. But here he was, stuttering a bit and just acting a little out of sorts. Still, I didn't pick up on it.

As we talked, Tracey stood up and came over to my side of the table. Taking my hand into his, he started telling me how much he loved me. As if it were a dream, his exact words escaped me. But he ended his speech with how he would be honored if I spent my life with him.

I watched as he reached behind his suit jacket and revealed a navy velvet box. He opened the top, and I saw a glistening round diamond ring.

Silence.

In reality, it was maybe only 45 seconds, it probably felt like a lifetime to Tracey. I was at a loss for words. Even though I knew it would happen, I'd put it out of my mind and thought it'd be another time. It was the first time I got proposed to. In my first marriage, we eloped. There was no declaration of love or romantic gesture. I was also startled because Tracey isn't a planner, but he had called ahead to the restaurant and hotel. When we got to our room, there were balloons, roses, champagne, and congratulatory signs. I couldn't have imagined this moment happening the way that it did. Tracey leaned into what I needed him to be. And I felt special in a way that I had never been before.

By midnight, Tracey was sleeping soundly. I could hear the crackling and boom of the fireworks outside our window. But, I couldn't close my eyes just yet. My cheeks were almost sore from smiling so much, but I didn't care. My husband, whom I had manifested for years, was finally right here beside me. In five months, I was going to say, "I do" to becoming Tracey's wife.

CHAPTER 12

It's Our Turn

Mom always wanted me to get married to the right person. She never said much about the men I dated over the years since she didn't think most of them were the best fit for me. Winston was an exception. She was fond of him but didn't love that we dated for so long. Mom would've been proud had it been someone who could bring me back to the Kingdom Hall and someone who had status – the latter being the cherry on top.

That is until she met Tracey.

By the fall of 2020, some significant things transpired between him and me that made me feel it was time he met my family. The first time was during a family Zoom meeting. Naturally, Mom had already heard quite a lot about Tracey, and I was eager to introduce them to each other. I could tell she certainly liked him. When she's fascinated with someone, she becomes extremely engaged with them. Her tone would change to that of curiosity. Then she'd start asking a lot of questions about the person. For instance, she'd say, "Tracey, tell me about yourself," and based on that answer, she'd ask more questions. She especially couldn't get over how handsome Tracey was. After the call, she texted me, "Tracey is muy guapo!" Ha!

SECOND ACT

About a month before the wedding, he and I flew to California, where everyone finally got to meet in person. Jubilation radiated throughout my body from the moment the plane touched down in San Francisco. As much as I loved Philly and the life Tracey and I were starting to build in New Jersey, Cali was always going to be home. I hadn't been back in a little over a year due to the pandemic, which was unusual for me. I'd fly there for anything, be it a wedding, a baby shower–heck, even a brunch. Seeing my family after so much time gave me the peace I'd been missing.

Tracey and I visited for a week. My girlfriend, Naimiah, gave me a "get to meet Tracey" shower, where he met a host of friends I consider more like family. He got to see my aunt, cousins, children, and of course, my mom. Out of the seven days, we spent four of them with mom. When we saw her, she was a bit thinner than she usually was. Early during COVID, she fell and broke her arm. So, I attributed her weight change to her injury and not going out much because of the virus, which she was very mindful of due to her age. Still, she was beaming, with her vibrant light brown sugar skin and hair shaped into a short, blonde afro. She didn't miss a beat. She still looked and acted youthful, sharp, and confident. Seeing Tracey, she wrapped her slender arms around him, swaying them both from side to side. When we hugged, I melted into her cozy embrace. We spent time at her three-bedroom apartment and talked for hours. Mom went through old pictures of me, Julian and Ashton. She even talked about my grandparents, particularly how admirable their marriage was. Mom recalled how she never heard her parents argue, and how Daddy Matthew always treated everyone kindly and cared for his family. I think mom sensed those qualities in Tracey. It's almost eerie how much he embodies

185

my grandfather. I especially remember how Daddy Matthew built Mama Opal a house in his hometown of Tyler, Texas, when the two retired. Today, Tracey is building me a home in Trenton, New Jersey.

"That's all I've ever wanted for Cheri," she said. Using my grandparents as inspiration, theirs was the type of marriage my mom envisioned for me. Noticing how jovial I was, in her way, she was giving her blessing of Tracey.

Momma may have been older, but she was just as spirited as she always was, especially when having intellectual debates. One time, as Tracey and I started making our way out to go back to our hotel, she initiated a discussion about young Black men being killed by the police.

"Tracey... Now, why can't men...you know...why can't they just surrender?" She probed.

Being the gentleman he is, Tracey was getting ready to respond when I jumped in.

"Mama, no. We do not have to play small to stay alive. It's never our fault that people kill and shoot us."

Just like when I was growing up, those exchanges were normal for us. I told Tracey how mom used to be a Black Panther. Even though she changed after converting to a Witness, that fire she had for having conversations on these deep topics (and taking somewhat of a contrarian position) never left. No matter how old she got, mom was still confident and could articulate her thoughts well. And just as he had won her over, Tracey was quite fond of her, too. He said he could see a lot of me in her and could tell that she was really proud of me.

It was such an incredible trip, but somehow, Tracey and I forgot to take pictures with momma. That was odd for us since we never missed an opportunity to capture a moment together. It's the only regret I have from our visit.

The next time I saw my mom, I had to say goodbye for the last time.

**

A week after our visit to California, Tracey and I were headed to Las Vegas. We'd been invited to a gala called Hope For Prisoners. Organized by a member of the JustLeadership USA (JL), it's a cohort of formerly incarcerated people who are leaders across the country, which Tracey is a part of. As we were getting off the plane, Julian called me.

"Hey Juju! We just landed in Vegas…"

I stopped when I heard her voice tremble.

"Mom…Gan Gan's sick… I don't know all the details but…"

Gagan was Julian's nickname for my mother.

Sick? What does she mean mamma's sick? How?

Not long after, I heard a beep interrupt us. Mom was calling me. That's when I knew it had to be something serious. She was calm, though her tone was a bit cerebral. I could tell she wanted to manage my emotions, as she was about to share some heavy information during one of the happiest times of my life. She was measured and thoughtful, as a mother who wanted to protect her only child. I could hear it in her voice. She told me her doctor found two masses on her liver but didn't know the extent of it. They would have to check it out to verify if they were cancerous. If so, we'd have to look at chemotherapy as a potential treatment. But what Mom told me next confirmed my deepest fear.

"No matter what happens to me, don't change anything with the wedding. Get married."

To this day, I don't know if my mom had been sick and didn't tell us or if that was the first time. But it was so fortuitous like she knew. And in my heart, I knew she was not going to make it.

I couldn't speak. It was as if I was underwater, gasping for air. I felt the weight of my body give out from under me, and the next thing I touched was the cold concrete of the airport air shuttle platform. With my hands as a barrier between my cheek and the floor, I let out a moan, like a wounded animal, as tears ran down my face. I could barely get any words out. I remember my phone lighting up. My girlfriend Naimah was trying to contact me. Tracey, his face damp, was on the floor beside me. Then, picking me up slightly, he held my face against his chest as we both cried out, in the airport.

A little less than a week later, Mom went into the hospital for a biopsy. She went in but never came out. From what I understand, air got to the cancer cell during the procedure, and started to spread throughout her body. The cancer attacked everything, and she never became coherent.

The doctor called me the night before Mother's Day.

"I don't know if your mom's going to make it through the night," he said, his voice heavy.

My heart stopped.

"I'm...surprised there's nobody here to see her," he added.

Because of COVID, the rest of the family and I weren't sure anyone could visit the hospital. Mom was there alone. But when I heard the doctor's prognosis, all I could feel was helplessness. Being across the country in New Jersey, there was nothing I could do except call everyone in California. Over the next several hours, hundreds of people went to see my mom. My friends. Her neighbors. Her people from the Kingdom Hall. Protocol be damned. But the hospital accommodated it.

Meanwhile, I couldn't fly out until that Thursday. The wedding was in less than two weeks. I was in the midst of planning a three-day event, and there were still so many important details to complete. Tracey was getting fitted for his tux the weekend of Mother's Day, and I was having mine for my dress on that Wednesday. Each day that passed was like living an out of body experience. I stayed connected to my phone, fielding calls all day and night, planning for the wedding and getting updates on my mom. Then the day before I was to leave, mom was moved to hospice.

My flight was set to leave on Thursday at 11 in the morning. But it got delayed until 6 that evening. I was racing against the clock, and every minute felt like an eternity. The hospice staff kept me abreast of mom's progress throughout the day. I finally made it to California around 9 p.m. and rushed to the hospice facility.

Walking into her room, Mom looked so peaceful lying in bed. This particular room was minimal. It reminded me of hospital rooms in the 50s and 60s, with a bed, a chair, and a nightstand—all wooden. There was a TV playing tranquil music in the room, and there was peace and serenity. Ashton's messages were all over the room, telling my mom how much she loved her. At the time, she was six months pregnant, and she left notes mentioning how Mom's new great-granddaughter, Oxean, was waiting for her. It was a reminder of her strength and a plea to hold on. I had time with my great-grandmother, as did my children. But my first grandbaby would never get the chance and I hated that. It was all so surreal. Our family was chatting and laughing hysterically in my mom's apartment a few weeks ago. I was in denial that this was happening, yet some part of me was still prepared for the inevitable. Climbing into bed, I cuddled with her.

As I stroked her face – her skin flawless – I told her how amazing she was. Not only as a mother to me but also with how supportive she was with Julian and Ashton. We lay together for an hour. As she took her last breath, I kept whispering in her ear how she did a great job.

"You don't have to hold on any longer than you have to, momma."

I'd made peace with my mother years before this moment. My years of coaching and self-discovery helped me resolve any resentment I had about my mother and her faith. I realized she did what she thought was best for me, as all parents do. I came to appreciate how remarkable she was in raising me to be who I am, and what she was to my children and her community of friends. I was thrilled that Tracey had the opportunity to meet her; she loved him. There was no reason for her to hang on. Knowing that she wasn't in any pain gave me solace. She could transition with ease. And because we had said everything we needed to say to each other before she passed, I was also at peace.

***

I don't regret any aspect of this journey – the highs and lows, the good, bad, and the crazy times. Despite the storms, I'm still here, sharing my story, because every experience prepared me to be right where I am now—as Mrs. Tracey Syphax, the proudest title I have ever carried.

If I had to pick the number one lesson I've learned, it's that life is to be lived. On the other side of fear are opportunities, experiences, people, and places. Moving past it truly expanded mine. If I hadn't, I wouldn't have started a new career in my mid-40s, moved across the country away from everyone and everything I knew, and dated online to find the love of my life. Creating my own limits led me to play small for years. I was just a portion of what I had the capacity to do and be. I wasn't taking up space, and I was trying to fit into places that didn't necessarily serve me. I used to be bogged down with worry, but life became completely different once I got over that. Shedding all those internal restrictions gave me the gift of liberation and empowered me to take on many risks.

I was once asked if I believed that women could have it all. And the answer is yes, I truly do. I think it all comes down to the story we tell ourselves. Take marriage, for instance. Sometimes the perception is that the demands of it may prevent you from doing other things. I used to have those reservations about marriage, too. But I've learned that when you're with the right person, they won't detract or subtract things from your life. They'll enhance it by pouring into you. Currently, my days are busy and long. As an executive with a thriving career, a growing coaching business, and sometimes as a personal assistant to my husband, Tracey is aware of where the limits need to be. He'll pull me to the side and say, "You're not doing anything this weekend. You're not working." When I'm trying to be a jack of all trades and the master of none, he's created capacity so that I can feel like I'm mastering all the things. And it's helped me understand how being married to the right person elevates you and expands your capacity.

When I reflect on finding love at a more mature time in life, again, it all comes back to what you tell yourself – that will dictate your ability to attract a quality partner. That may sound nefarious in a way, but I've lived it and know it can happen. Available men are abundant out there. People are getting married every day, and it is not age bound, contrary to what the media or your girlfriends tell you. It is by design. It's easy to think of our age as a valid reason to stay stagnant or to lose our spark. But when you stop and think about it, you know yourself so much better at this point in your life. There's so much that's influenced who you are. You've had some experiences. You've had some wins, so you know what you like. And you've had some losses, so you know what you don't like. Most of us have confidence at a certain age that we didn't have when we first started. And that puts us in a prime position to really attract the person who is for us.

At the age of 52, I know so much more. I know what I want sexually. I know how to talk to a man differently than before because I've managed people. I also understand how being an only child impacts the man in my life and me. Now, I can communicate that to him as opposed to when I was young, selfish, and lacked self-awareness. There are so many things that I know about myself, and I'm much better equipped to have conversations in a very fruitful and meaningful way. As a mature woman, I can speak to what my needs and desires are. You can meet them, or you don't have to. Either way, I'm good, and I'm fine. I think that's why my soulmate prayer was so beneficial. It was about how I wanted a man to make me feel – joy, satisfaction, peace, and eagerness. And that's what I believe maturity of age brings. It's the best place to attract the love you desire.

But it all starts with the relationship we have with ourselves. To my fellow women of color, we need healing, first and foremost. Many of us have so much past hurt that we haven't fully reconciled with. There's so much trauma that we've had, both culturally and socially in this country and in relationships. Not only with men but with our families, parents, and work. Some of the distress our parents passed down to us needs to be unpacked, and it hasn't been. We look to our family so much for validation. Often, we think what they do and say is gospel without stopping to think about how they were informed. Who raised them? And did those who raised our parents have unhealed experiences that they passed down? Ultimately, we didn't choose our family.

Sometimes, we may have unrealistic expectations of our parents' capacity to love, grow, and nurture us. If they didn't feel love, it may be difficult for them to show it. There are so many complexities to the human experience, and I've realized that our parents are people, just like we are. They are not mythical superheroes with all of the answers. They have issues just like we do and, depending on the generation they grew up in, had less resources to help them cope. They were figuring out life while trying to raise a whole human. We must learn to make peace and forgive the areas where our parents may have fallen short or their inability to nurture us the way we desire. But that also means creating boundaries with them. Just because it's our mother or father does not mean they are excused from being emotionally manipulative or abusive.

Along the way, I had to unpack my parents' influence on my life. Understanding their behavior made me realize how I'd been impacted, and how it was showing up in my relationships. My father's infidelities. My mother's pride. For her, Momma Opal and Daddy Matthew were great parents. He was a provider, and she was a wonderful spouse. But they didn't show much affection towards each other. It's something a lot of Black families don't do. As a result, my mother was not as affectionate or gave me affirming words. She was also the youngest, and in some ways, I believe she felt the need to prove herself and show how smart she was. It's most likely where that competitive spirit came from and probably contributed to her inability to concede to me or tell me how proud of me she was. I wanted her validation. No matter what I did, it felt like I could never measure up. Ultimately, I had to decide to forgive and accept her for whom she was, while also becoming secure in who I am. I had to recognize that mom and I are different people. (And do you know, one day, she finally told me, "You know, I'm proud of you.")

Our lack of self-esteem and understanding of our values also stems from not having enough people telling us how amazing we are. Yes, we're often called the strong Black woman, but I don't know if that's a compliment. We are multifaceted. We have a multitude of depth and dimension. So much ingenuity, class, and sass. So many wonderful, positive things. But we feel unappreciated. We feel rejected and unprotected. And that comes out in our relationships. It shows up in how we view our self-worth. We have this need to live this trope of, 'I can do it all. I got to have this cape on. I don't need no man.' We are the most educated group in this country, but we've also been taught to wear that on our chest as a badge of honor. We tie our worthiness to status, whether it's education, career, or finances. I'd never tell you to dumb yourself down, but we don't have to lead with what we've accomplished to be worthy of a man who will love who we are.

In most things, as with love, there's a process to go through before reaching the desired result. You can't open new doors with old keys. When I changed my relationship with myself, everything else shifted. The first step is to be aware of where you are as a person and fully accept it. Whether you are divorced, have children, or had several bad relationships in the past. However dreadful it may seem, start with accepting yourself. Once you've done that, then it's time to make a plan. What do you want to get better at? Identify those things you want to improve on and start one at a time. Many of us struggle with feelings of unworthiness and lack of self-confidence. But we set the example for how people will treat us by how we treat ourselves. Are you talking to yourself positively? Do you look at yourself in the mirror and say, "I'm beautiful. I love myself. And hell yeah, I'm amazing!" Also, be honest about what you want. If you desire to get married, communicate that to prospective partners. You don't have to pretend that you're too cool to say what you want. The person who wants the same will find it magnetic. Developing your self-worth will ultimately help you attract the right individual into your life. When we do the inner work and tap into our hearts, we can attract absolutely anything.

I know it's hard for us to believe that we are worthy. But I want you to know that you are beautifully crafted and wonderfully made. Whomever you are and whatever you want, own it! Gracefully. Learn from your mistakes. Be accountable. Apply the knowledge. Embrace the experience. Continue to elevate and make yourself better. And life will unfold for you in a miraculously amazing way!

Acknowledgements:

I want to thank everyone I have encountered along this journey. In some way, shape, or form, you have directly, or indirectly influenced this amazing Second Act. Some are noted in the book, but for those of you who aren't, it does not mean your impact was not significant. That includes my in-laws, friends, coaches, co-workers, mentors, mentees, associates, and anyone who has crossed my path, you are appreciated. No matter the significance, it ultimately got me here.

To my grandparents, those special individuals who were not only the stability for me and my parents, but filled my life with so much love, wisdom, and joy.

To my parents, both gone too soon, you are why I am. I don't have words to articulate what you mean to me. The depth of grief I experience has so much to do with you not being here today to see how deeply Tracey loves me, and the beautiful life we experience everyday. It is EXACTLY what you envisioned for me. You did that. You both poured everything you had into me, and gave me everything I needed to soar. I am honoring your memory by doing just that, soaring.

To my three amigas, the trifecta, the treacherous three, Robin, Tantani, and Naimah, thank you for being on this CRAZY journey with me. If I die tomorrow, I would have LIVED life to the fullest, for the most part, because of you. I couldn't love you deeper if we were blood related. Thank you for being all the things a sister-friend needed to be, when it was easy and hard.

Julian and Ashton, WOW. What a wonderful ride this has been. When we first started, I didn't imagine the places we would have gone. Thank you for being my first teachers, my inspirations, my motivations, and my WHY. I am still your number one fan, and hope I make you as proud of me as I have been blessed to be of you.

Last, but definitely not least, and ironically, the last significant person to come into my life, Tracey. What can I say about you, my love? You never cease to amaze me. When I think of where you have been, and where you are today, I get chills. The depth in which you love me, care for me, and provide for me is something I have yearned for all of my life. It delights my heart to know my mother loved the love you showed me. Let's keep living, loving, shining, and thriving. I love you, Black Man. Team Syphax, the Super Bowl Champions of LOVE.

CPSIA information can be obtained
at www.ICGtesting.com
Printed in the USA
LVHW110625090223
739018LV00003B/21